Contents

CONTRIBUTING AUTHORS

David Appel
Economic and Social Research
  Department
National Council on Compensation
  Insurance
New York, NY 10119

Philip S. Borba
Economic and Social Research
  Department
National Council on Compensation
  Insurance
New York, NY 10119

Richard J. Butler
Department of Economics
Brigham Young University
Provo, Utah 85602

John F. Burton, Jr.
School of Industrial and Labor Relations
Cornell University
Ithaca, New York 14853

J. David Cummins
Department of Insurance
The Wharton School
University of Pennsylvania
Philadelphia, Pennsylvania 19104

Neil A. Doherty
Department of Insurance
The Wharton School
University of Pennsylvania
Philadelphia, Pennsylvania 19104

Scott E. Harrington
College of Business Administration
University of South Carolina
Columbia, SC 29208

H. Allan Hunt
Employment Research
Upjohn Institute
300 S. Westnedge Avenue
Kalamazoo, Michigan 49007

vii

William G. Johnson
Deparment of Economics
Health Studies Program
The Maxwell School
Syracuse University
Syracuse, New York 13210

Alan B. Krueger
Princeton University
Princeton, NJ 08544

James Lambrinos
Program in Health Systems
   Administration
Union College
Schenectady, New York 12065

Harris Schlesinger
College of Business Administration
University of Alabama
Tuscaloosa, Alabama 35487

Emilio C. Venezian
Department of Business Administration
Rutgers University
Newark, New Jersey 07102

John D. Worrall
Department of Economics
Rutgers University
New Brunswick, New Jersey 08903

Workers' Compensation Insurance Pricing

Current Programs and Proposed Reforms

Huebner International Series on Risk, Insurance, and Economic Security

J. David Cummins, Editor
The Wharton School
University of Pennsylvania
Philadelphia, Pennsylvania, U.S.A.

Series Advisors:

Dr. Phelim P. Boyle,
University of Waterloo, Canada
Dr. Jean Lemaire,
Universite Libre de Bruxelles, Belguim
Dr. Akohiko Tsuboi,
Kagawa University, Japan
Dr. Richard Zeckhauser,
Harvard University, U.S.A.

Previously published books in the series:

Cummins, J. David; Smith, Barry D.;
    Vance, R. Neil; VanDerhei, Jack L.:
    Risk Classification in Life Insurance
Mintel, Judith: *Insurance Rate Litigation*
Cummins, J. David: *Strategic Planning and
    Modeling in Property–Liability Insurance*
Lemaire, Jean: *Automobile Insurance:
    Actuarial Models*
Rushing, William A.: *Social Functions and
    Economic Aspects of Health Insurance*
Cummins, J. David and Harrington, Scott E.:
    Fair Rate of Return in Property–Liability Insurance

The objective of the series is to publish original research and
advanced textbooks dealing with all major aspects of risk bearing
and economic security. The emphasis is on books that will be of
interest to an international audience. Interdisciplinary topics as well
as those from traditional disciplines such as economics, risk and
insurance, and actuarial science are within the scope of the series.
The goal is to provide an outlet for imaginative approaches to
problems in both the theory and practice of risk and economic
security.

Workers' Compensation Insurance Pricing

Current Programs and Proposed Reforms

Editors:
Philip S. Borba and David Appel
National Council on Compensation Insurance
One Penn Plaza
New York, New York 10119

1988 Kluwer Academic Publishers
Boston / Dordrecht / London

Distributors for North America:
Kluwer Academic Publishers
101 Philip Drive
Assinippi Park
Norwell, Massachusetts 02061 USA

Distributors for the UK and Ireland:
Kluwer Academic Publishers
Falcon House, Queen Square
Lancaster LA1 1RN, UNITED KINGDOM

Distributors for all other countries:
Kluwer Academic Publishers
Distribution Centre
Post Office Box 322
3300 AH Dordrecht, THE NETHERLANDS

Library of Congress Cataloging-in-Publication Data

Workers compensation insurance pricing.
  (Huebner international series on risk, insurance,
and economic security)
  Bibliography: p.
  Included index.
  1. Workers' compensation—Rites and tables.
I. Appel, David, 1950–   . II. Borba, Philip S.
III. Series.
HD7103.6.W67   1988   368.4'1011   88–1239
ISBN 0-89838-268-8

Printed in the United States of America

Workers' Compensation Insurance Pricing

Current Programs and Proposed Reforms

1 COSTS AND PRICES OF WORKERS' COMPENSATION INSURANCE

David Appel
Philip S. Borba

Workers' compensation insurance provides medical payments and cash benefits to over seven million injured workers per year. As such, it is probably the largest social insurance program in the nation after Social Security. In the private market alone, employers paid approximately $20 billion in 1986 to insure their obligations under the various state workers' compensation statutes. Add to that the coverage provided by the federal government, state funds, and self-insurance, and the total expenditures for compensation of injury arising "out of, or in the course of employment" must exceed $30 billion. Given its size and scope, workers' compensation insurance must be the most under-researched social insurance program in the nation.

Although it has largely escaped the attention of academic research, the workers' compensation insurance industry has not avoided the close scrutiny of consumers, insurers or regulators in this decade. Once a rather predictable line of coverage in the property–casualty insurance industry, workers' compensation insurance has recently become one of the more contentious and unsettled components of the insurance environment. While issues of availability have largely been avoided (in contrast to the considerable concerns in other property–casualty lines), the questions of affordability, cost containment, solvency, equity and adequacy of benefits, and accuracy of pricing have merited significant attention.[1]

1

It is against this backdrop that this book was produced. The National Council on Compensation Insurance (NCCI), the nation's foremost workers' compensation research and rate-making organization, has long been interested in eliciting quality research in areas of concern to workers' compensation insurance. In previous years we have addressed the demand-side of the workers' compensation system, concentrating on benefit adequacy, equity, and utilization issues.[2] In this volume, we turn our attention to supply-side concerns, addressing the current status of the pricing and production of workers' compensation insurance.

Although the institutional arrangements surrounding the production and consumption of workers' compensation insurance have been in place for decades, the system has also undergone considerable strain in recent years. In a recent paper, Berkowitz and Berkowitz (1985) discussed challenges to the system that have arisen through the years but that relate predominantly to the benefit side of the program. In this volume, we direct our attention more to the pricing and production of this insurance coverage, which have also been the subject of widespread discussion and debate. Indeed, the questions of equity and efficiency are every bit as significant on the pricing side as they are on the benefits side.

Before reviewing our principal findings, we will provide in this chapter a brief description of the benefits and pricing procedures that concern workers' compensation insurance. First we will review the coverage and benefit provisions under the various state workers' compensation laws; then we will provide a broad overview of the current pricing system; and finally we will discuss the findings presented in this volume.

Workers' Compensation Insurance

Workers' compensation insurance provides for medical coverage and wage replacement for losses from injuries arising "out of, or in the course of employment." The system arose in the early decades of the twentieth century as part of a well-known "quid pro quo," in which employees relinquished their rights to tort action against employers in exchange for swift and certain settlement of their claims for industrial accidents. Provision of this coverage is compulsory in 47 states, and elective in three others, although provisions in the laws make the coverage virtually mandatory in these jurisdictions as well.

Employers can secure their obligations under the various workers' compensation statutes in several ways. Most common is the purchase of insurance in the private market from insurers licensed to sell workers' compensation coverage. In addition to private insurance, 18 states operate state insurance funds; in 12 of these jurisdictions, the state competes with private insurers, while in the other six the state monopoly is the exclusive source of coverage. As an alternative to private insurers or the state funds, employers who meet certain requirements may elect to self-insure in 47 jurisdictions, usually by posting a bond demonstrating the ability to meet statutory obligations under the workers' compensation laws. Finally, group self-insurance is permitted in 25 states. Group self-insurance allows small employers, typically within the same industry, to pool their risks.

Regardless of the method for securing the liability, the employer is responsible for the statutory benefits which accrue to an employee upon injury. Those benefits include medical costs, which are fully covered in every jurisdiction, and indemnity, or wage-loss, payments, which vary considerably across states. Injuries are classified into one of five categories, depending upon the nature and extent of disability:

1. *Medical only:* injuries that require medical treatment, and result in work absences less than the statutory waiting period (usually between three and seven days);
2. *Temporary Total:* injuries that are totally disabling, but from which full recovery and return to work is expected;
3. *Permanent Partial:* injuries which, even after a healing period, result in a permanent impairment, functional disability, or loss of earning capacity;
4. *Permanent Total:* injuries which cause a permanent and total inability to return to work;
5. *Fatal:* injuries which result in the death of the worker.

Table 1-1 shows the distribution of injuries and costs incurred by private workers' compensation insurers and competitive state funds for the most recent available policy period.

Workers' compensation insurance was designed specifically to reduce the uncertainties associated with industrial illnesses and injuries. The no-fault nature of the arrangement relieves the injured worker of the burden of proof in demonstrating employer negligence, while also eliminating the traditional common-law defenses employers had routinely used to avoid liability. Workers' compensation insurance enables injured workers to obtain the treatment and rehabilitation necessary to return to work, while providing income support during the recovery period. In the case of the more serious, long-term injuries, the system also provides continuing support that recompenses workers for lost wages.

Table 1-1.   Claim Cost and Percentage Distribution by Claim Severity: Ultimate
Report Basis, Countrywide Results

Claim Type	Average Cost ($)	Percent of Total Cost (%)	Percent of All Claims (%)	Percent of Indemnity Claims (%)
Death	$103,524	4.4	0.0	0.4
Permanent Total Disability	170,673	5.7	0.0	0.3
Permanent Partial Disability				
Major	62,031	44.9	1.1	6.0
Minor	8,833	17.8	3.2	16.7
Temporary Total Disability	2,319	21.4	14.4	76.6
Medical Only	157	5.8	81.2	
All Claims	2,012	100.0	100.0	100.0

From the National Council on Compensation Insurance (NCCI), countrywide results. Frequency percentages exclude Delaware, Massachusetts, and Pennsylvania. Results also exclude certain state funds. Policy years (the period in which the policy is in effect) vary by state. For additional information, contact NCCI Actuarial Information Services.

While these are laudable objectives, we recognize that their achievement is not necessarily costless. In the idealized world of perfectly competitive markets, with homogeneous preferences, complete and costless information, perfect certainty, and zero transactions cost, workers would be paid compensating wage differentials for job risk equal to the expected costs of workplace injury. Under these conditions, workers and firms would sort themselves in such a way as to maximize the utility of workers and the profits of firms. The optimal amount of safety investment would be undertaken and the optimal number of injuries would occur. Unfortunately, we do not live in such as Coase-type world.[3] The world is uncertain, information and transactions are costly, preferences vary and markets are imperfect. Into such a world the government enters, mandating a plethora of social insurance programs including workers' compensation. The impacts of such programs can be substantial.

Although the costs of workers' compensation insurance depend on the benefit structure and behavior of injured workers, the price paid for the coverage is (at least nominally) borne by the employer. The next section in this introductory chapter reviews the procedures by which these costs are incorporated into the price for workers' compensation insurance coverage. We include a discussion of the basic actuarial procedures used to develop the manual rates and various rating systems, as well as the manner by which the manual rates are adjusted to obtain the competitive-market cost of coverage.

Workers' Compensation Pricing

While conceptually quite straightforward, the pricing of workers' compensation is, in practice, a rather complicated matter.[4] As might be expected, different types of employment have differing expected costs of illness and injury. Therefore, in order to meet the typical statutory requirement that "rates be neither excessive, inadequate or unfairly discriminatory," rates must vary by type of employment. Furthermore, as the regulation of benefits is jurisdictionally a statewide matter, rates will vary by state as well. A very brief discussion of the pricing program follows.

Workers' compensation premiums must cover the expected losses and expenses allocable to the policies written while the rates are in effect. Both equity and efficiency require that this holds true in the aggregate (i.e., at the statewide level), and at the level of the individual insured as well. The failure to adhere to this principle can cause unintended interjurisdictional, interindustry and interfirm cross-subsidization, which can have far-reaching and adverse implications. As a result, the pricing procedure is three-tiered: initially the average statewide price level is computed, followed by adjustments for individual industries, and then for individual firms.

The first step in the process is the assessment of rate adequacy at the state level. Total premium volume at current rates is compared to total expected losses and expenses at current benefit levels to determine the average rate change for the state. The average rate change is then distributed to the approximately 600 individual classifications in two stages. First, each classification is assigned to one of three industry groups—manufacturing, construction, and all other. The premium change is initially distributed to the three groups, and then to the individual class codes within each group.[5] The prices that result from this procedure are known as "manual rates."

The manual rates represent the average loss and expense cost per unit of exposure (i.e., per $100 of payroll) for each of the classifications. As benefits vary across states, and as the distribution (i.e., frequency and severity) of injuries varies across types of employment, these rates can vary considerably. For example, the maximum rate in a state will routinely exceed the minimum by a factor of 100, and in extreme cases can exceed the minimum by a factor of 1000. (Expressed as a percentage, the rates can range from .1 to 100 percent of payroll.) In addition, controlling for the wage distribution and mix of employment, the average manual rate can vary across states by a factor of ten.

After the manual rate is established, individual firm prices may be further adjusted through the application of a number of mandatory and voluntary programs. The most significant of these, from the equity and efficiency perspective, are mandatory experience rating and premium discounts.

Experience Rating

The first adjustment to an employer's manual rate is the mandatory NCCI Experience Rating Plan (ERP). For every employer generating an annual manual premium (the product of the manual rate and payroll) in excess of the state minimum, the ERP produces a modification factor that is applied multiplicatively to the manual rate.[6] The modification factor is basically a weighted average of the employer's actual losses for the most recent three years for which data are available and the expected losses for a typical employer in the classification. The weight attached to an employer's experience increases proportionally for larger employers. An employer with manual premiums in excess of the self-rating point is perfectly experience-rated— that is, the premium is determined solely by the firm's own experience.[7] In contrast, the experience of employers with relatively small premiums is accorded a low credibility (i.e., low statistical significance), and the premium is determined primarily by the experience of other employers in the classification.

Currently, ten to fifteen percent of all employers are large enough to be subject to the NCCI Experience Rating Plan.[8] However, experience-rated employers account for approximately ninety percent of all employees covered by workers' compensation insurers in NCCI jurisdictions. The relatively low threshold for inclusion in the NCCI ERP is demonstrated by observing that an employer for whom the manual rate is $2.50 per $100 of payroll will be covered by the ERP if the payroll exceeds $100,000. Stated another way, given the average manual rate in manufacturing, an employer with as few as four full-time employees earning the average weekly wage in manufacturing would qualify for the experience rating.

Premium Discounts

The manual premium after modification for experience rating is known as "standard premium." The second mandatory program, the premium discount plan, then adjusts the standard premium to reflect fixed costs in the insurance production process and economies of scale in the servicing of large risks. The NCCI Discount Plan reduces the premium volume for most employers with an annual standard premium in excess of $5000.[9] There are two discount plans available, depending upon whether the insurer is a stock or nonstock company.[10] The discount plan typically used by stock companies ranges from a ten-percent discount for premiums in excess of $5000 and less than $100,000, to a fourteen-percent discount for premiums in excess of $1,000,000. The nonstock plan discounts range from three percent to seven percent, principally due to the fact that nonstock companies typically pay larger dividends to policyholders.

In addition to the mandatory Experience Rating Plan and Discount Plan, there are several other, voluntary, pricing programs by which premiums are adjusted to reflect more accurately the expected costs of workers' compensation insurance coverage. Each program is intended to be responsive to the circumstances of an individual employer, and thus to enhance the equity of the pricing system.

Retrospective Rating

Retrospective rating refers to a set of voluntary plans that tie an individual insured's price directly to the costs it generates, with prespecified minimum and maximum limitations. Although they vary in their specific provisions, each of the plans provides for a basic premium that compensates the insurer for the expenses associated with the administrative and overhead costs and for the loss limits specified in the policy. One of the most familiar of these plans, known as the *paid loss retro*, charges an insured only as losses are paid under the policy. Note that retrospective rating is quite different from the experience rating program: not only is it elective, but more importantly it establishes a variable cost for insurance, depending upon the losses incurred under the policy. Thus it is prospective, as opposed to experience rating, which offers the insured a guaranteed cost that is adjusted based on the predictive value of the individual risk's historical experience.

Deviations and Schedule Rating

Deviations are flat percentage adjustments in the standard premiums that must be filed with the state insurance regulatory agency by individual insurers. Deviations apply to all insureds covered by the insurer in the state, and although they may increase or decrease premiums, deviations typically reduce the standard premium by ten to twenty-five percent. Deviations are permitted in approximately three-quarters of the 45 states in which workers' compensation insurance rates are not administered by a monopolistic state fund.

Schedule rating is a system by which debits or credits are applied to an insured's standard premium to reflect the potential for cost saving or generating activities on the part of the specific risk. Typical reasons for granting schedule credits may be the presence of machine guards on hazardous equipment or a safety training course for employees. In contrast to the use of deviations, a schedule rating plan does not have to apply to all risks covered by the insured. Schedule rating plans have been approved in approximately one-half of the 45 states in which workers' compensation insurance rates are not administered by a monopolistic state fund.

The application of the Experience Rating Plan, deviations, schedule rating plans, retrospective rating plans, and premium discounts produces the *net earned premium*, which is the amount that an employer is charged for the workers' compensation insurance coverage. In addition, the real cost of coverage can be reduced by deferring a portion of the premium until a later date through a waiver of the deposit-premium requirement.

Policyholder Dividends

All of the programs described above are *front-end* price adjustments—that is, they provide for guaranteed adjustments to the cost of insurance coverage, and are part of the contractual arrangement between employer and insurer. Policyholder dividends, the final cost-reduction program, is *back-end*, occurring after the expiration of the policy.

Although policyholders cannot be guaranteed dividends at the time the policy is written, most dividend plans provide an estimated dividend percentage based upon the premium size, loss results, and expenses for an individual employer. Furthermore, insurers are not required to file dividend plans with the state regulatory authorities, and the actual payment of dividends is not determined until the company's loss results are reviewed by its board of directors. In a few states, discount plans have not been approved and, consequently, dividend plans are quite generous. Dividend plans have been an important means by which insurers have engaged in aggressive pricing competition.

Dividend plans can be grouped into two broad categories: (1) the relatively generous plans of mutual companies, as well as stock companies that use *participating rating* plans, and (2) the less generous *nonparticipating rating* plans used by many stock companies. During 1985, nonparticipating stock companies wrote $6.9 billion in workers' compensation coverage, while participating stock companies wrote $5.6 billion and mutual companies wrote $4.1 billion. Although the nonparticipating stock companies were originally not expected to pay policyholders' dividends, competition from participating stock and mutual companies has forced nonparticipating stock companies to offer plans that provide relatively sizeable dividends. During 1985, nonparticipating stock companies returned 7.9% of premium to insureds, compared to 10.3% and 11.0% for participating stock and mutual companies, respectively.

Equity and Efficiency in Workers' Compensation

The traditional standard for workers' compensation rate-making is that rates be "neither excessive, inadequate or unfairly discriminatory."[11] In order to adhere to this regulatory standard, a number of significant equity and efficiency issues must be addressed. First, prices must accurately reflect the medical and indemnity costs resulting from workplace illness and injury. Second, prices to the individual insured should accurately reflect the expected marginal cost that risk imposes on the system. Finally, the funds generated by the pricing programs must be adequate to insure the solvency and solidity of the carriers, so they may discharge their obligations under the various benefit programs. Each chapter of this volume relates directly to one or more of these areas.

Estimation of Costs

Beginning in the early 1970s, with the advent of the National Commission on State Workmens' Compensation Laws, the question of benefit adequacy and equity began to be addressed in a forthright fashion. The Commission issued a number of recommendations, of which 19 were deemed essential, with nine relating to the necessity for the state workers' compensation systems to improve the level of benefits payable to injured workers.[12] This also spawned an investigation into the incentives and disincentives created by the benefit system, which has become one of the most fruitful areas of research in the economics of workers' compensation.

Although there was initially some disagreement about the nature and extent of the potential work disincentives created by the payment of workers' compensation benefits, in recent years there appears to be a growing uniformity of opinion on this matter. Many researchers, using different models, data sets and time periods, have found substantial increases in costs associated with increased workers' compensation benefits.[13] Moreover, these cost increases are both direct (i.e., due to a higher level of benefits payable for all injuries) and indirect, or induced (due to increased injury frequency and severity associated with higher benefit levels).

This research holds more than an academic interest to insurers. The accurate estimation of benefit costs is the single most important characteristic of an acceptable pricing program. Since there is evidence that the structure of a benefits program creates incentives to assume more on-the-job risk, to increase the rate at which claims are filed, or to increase the duration of disability for the claims that are filed, insurers are obliged to take these incentives into consideration in their cost estimates. Butler and Worrall have made a substantial contribution to the research in this area. In the present volume they provide new estimates of the increase in claims costs associated with increased benefit levels, using recently developed maximum likelihood estimation techniques. This methodology permits tests for alternative claims-generation models, while controlling for heterogeneity across both workers and firms.

Using data on risks from 38 states in 11 classifications, Butler and Worrall estimate the distribution of workers' compensation claims costs under a number of alternative distributional assumptions. Although they are unable to select a claims-generation model, they do report strong evidence that costs are systematically related to wages, benefits, and experience rating. Specifically, Butler and Worrall find that a ten-percent increase in benefits increases liabilities by approximately fifteen percent—an impact which is remarkably similar to the estimates produced from previous studies. In addition, they report a significant negative relationship between costs and both wages and firm size—findings which also confirm the results of considerable previous research. As hypothesized, workers and firms respond to the incentive in the system.

While Butler and Worrall describe the observed variation in claims costs, Lambrinos and Johnson present a proposal that may serve to remove some of the variability in the costs of certain types of claims. Lambrinos and Johnson propose a prospective payment system for workers' compensation insurance benefits that is modeled on the diagnosis-related groups (DRGs) used in the Medicare system for hospital reimbursement. The premise of the proposal is that a system in which payments are known in advance provides greater incentives to control costs than a system in which all costs are paid retrospectively.

The Lambrinos and Johnson proposal would provide injured workers with temporary total or permanent partial claims with an indemnity benefit that is uniform for all claims with similar characteristics. They argue that this may improve the equity of benefits disbursed under workers' compensation while improving the efficiency of benefit systems and, hopefully, reducing the escalating losses associated with temporary total and permanent partial claims.

A particularly troublesome problem that has developed over the last two decades concerns the benefits for, and pricing of, occupational diseases covered by workers' compensation insurance. Many occupational diseases are costly and may, in part, be attributable to off-the-job exposures. Both costliness and questions concerning compensability present serious problems for pricing workers' compensation insurance, particularly for exposures that may be susceptible to a high frequency of occupational disease claims. In the present volume, Schlesinger and Venezian address many of the problems associated with implementing a benefit structure for occupational disease claims, especially those concerning the assignment of liability. Included in the discussion are the issues of multiple causes and sources, multiple exposures that do not necessarily imply additive contributions to the disease, long latency, the failure of claimants to take proper pre-disease precautions or post-disease treatment, and the failure of employers to provide the safest working conditions.

Equity in Pricing

We previously noted that an increase in workers' compensation insurance benefits can be expected to increase the frequency of workplace injuries and the duration of disability periods. However, the impact of the increased claim frequency and severity will be partially mitigated by the increased incentives on the part of employers to reduce workers' compensation insurance losses. Generally speaking, experience rating plans increase (decrease) the premium for employers with worse- (better-) than-average loss experience. Consequently, if an increase in benefits causes a deterioration in an employer's loss experience, the return from investing in workplace safety will be improved. Given that the degree of an employer's experience in the insurance premium increases with the size of the employer, the incentives to provide safer working conditions are greater for larger employers.

In a recent study, Ruser (1985) tested this hypothesis using models which specified injury frequency as a function of a number of variables, including a benefit–size interaction term. If experience rating is effective, the sign on the coefficient for the benefit–size variable should be negative; that is, the increase in frequency associated with higher benefit levels should be smaller in larger firms. The hypothesized explanation, as noted above, is that as firm size increases, employers bear a greater share of the costs of workplace injury due to more perfect experience rating. Thus, larger employers have a greater incentive to reduce workplace injury as benefits increase.

In the present volume, Worrall and Butler extend this research by evaluating whether experience rating plans cause employers to control the seriousness of workplace injuries. Similar to Ruser, Worrall and Butler include a benefit–size interaction variable, but perform the analysis separately for the frequencies of permanent partial and temporary total types of workers' compensation insurance claims. Worrall and Butler report that, holding benefits constant, a ten-percent increase in the size of the employer leads to a 4.95-percent decrease in the permanent partial injury rate, and a 1.55-percent decrease in the temporary total injury rate.

Harrington presents a more general discussion concerning the relationship between a firm's size and loss experience. He begins with familiar characterizations of a firm's standard premium and actual loss experience, and proceeds to impute the effect of the experience rating and primary-to-total losses into the premium and loss expressions. The conceptual model concludes with a losses-to-standard-premium ratio that, with imperfect experience rating for some firms, is shown to be inversely related to the size of the firm.

In the empirical analysis, Harrington uses aggregate state data on actual losses and standard earned premiums for employers arranged into 16 premium size groups. He computes actual-to-expected loss ratios for each size group and then shows that, for three of the four states in the analysis, the actual-to-expected loss ratio is inversely related to firm size. The implications of these results are significant in at least two respects. First, they are consistent with the findings of Ruser and Worrall and Butler that experience rating creates incentives for improved loss experience. Second, they suggest that the experience of large employers should not be accorded an undue weight in the computation of statewide workers' compensation manual rates. Given that insurers compete for employers with low actual-to-expected loss ratios (e.g., premium discounts, rate deviations, dividends, aggressive service programs), equitable and adequate rates may be more likely to be obtained by increasing reliance on the experience of small employers.

The chapters by Harrington and Worrall and Butler address the question of the impact of experience rating on individual employers. Indeed, although experience rating is seen to provide incentives for loss containment, the insurance industry has always viewed the program as one primarily intended to produce equity in pricing, by more closely tying an individual risk's price to expected costs. This aspect of the program directly addresses the requirement that rates should not be unfairly discriminatory.

In addition to equity across firms, another issue of importance is interjurisdictional differences in pricing. Differences in benefit provisions, the industrial composition of the work force, and the adequacy of rate levels present many troublesome problems for comparing workers' compensation insurance rate levels across states. Over the last 20 years, John F. Burton, Jr., has performed extensive studies concerning interstate differences in the employers' costs of workers' compensation insurance. In the present volume, H. Allan Hunt, Alan B. Kruegar, and Burton provide an important extension to the literature with an evaluation of the Michigan open competition rating statute. Effective January 1, 1983, a Michigan insurer must apply its own expense loading and trend factor to the advisory pure premium rates published by the NCCI. Furthermore, a Michigan insurer is permitted under the open competition statute to use its own experience rating formula, expense and loss constants, and premium discounts.

The Hunt, Kruegar, and Burton study is principally concerned with the average rates employers have been charged since the introduction of open competition rating compared to the simulated rates that employers would have been charged under the prior approval rating system. For 1983 through 1985, they estimate the average manual rate that employer would have paid under the pre-1983 prior approval system and adjust the average rate for the impact of expense and loss constants, experience rating modifications and retrospective rating, premium discounts, and dividends to policyholders. Hunt, Kruegar, and Burton also use the manual rates that employers were charged—adjusted for experience rating, premium discounts, and other pricing plans—to derive the average employer's cost of coverage under the open competition statute. The results suggest that the Michigan open competition statute reduced the costs of workers' compensation insurance for the state's employers by approximately 25%, 30%, and 10–15% in 1983 through 1985, respectively. Although the evidence suggests that employers' costs were reduced during the three years following the effective date of the statute, the authors are cautious over whether the cost savings will persist. At a minimum, the authors conclude that, even though the cost savings may not persist, Michigan employers benefited from the savings attributable to the "shock effect" caused by the introduction of the open rating system.

Insurer Solvency

A recurring concern of insurance regulators and policyholders is that the insurer will be able to assume the liabilities covered by the insurance contract. The National Association of Insurance Commissioners annually performs the Insurance Regulatory Information System (IRIS) tests, which use 11 standards to evaluate the financial solidity of an insurer. In addition, the A.M. Best Company annually publishes the *Key Rating Guide*, in which analysts assign a letter grade that can be used to evaluate the solidity of an insurer.

Despite this regulatory oversight and the availability of private market information, there were 58 insolvencies among property–casualty insurers over the 1984–1986 period, several of which involved carriers with significant workers' compensation exposure. The number and magnitude of these insolvencies is unusual; in the three previous years only 19 insolvencies were reported among property–casualty insurers.

Practically speaking, an employer covered by a workers' compensation insurance policy is protected from insolvency of the insurer through a guaranty fund that is administered by a state regulatory agency. These funds require that solvent insurers assume the liabilities of other carriers in the event of insolvency. They are typically funded on a postassessment basis; that is, the remaining, solvent insurers are assessed a fixed percentage of premium volume such that the total assessment covers the unfunded liabilities of the insolvent carrier. While such a procedure protects insureds, it can also create incentives among insurers to bear more risk, both in their underwriting and investment portfolios. This occurs because the higher returns associated with riskier activities accrue to the insurer, while the insolvency risk is shifted to the industry as a whole.[14] In this volume, Cummins presents an alternative methodology for determining guaranty fund premiums that attempts to mitigate the incentive to increase risk.

Cummins recommends a risk-based premium for insurance guaranty funds that would represent the value of the fund's promise to pay the excess of the firm's liabilities over assets in the event of insolvency. The value of such a promise is implicitly the expected cost of an insolvency. To determine its fair price, both the assets and liabilities of the insurer are modelled as diffusion processes; an insolvency occurs if liabilities drift above assets during the contract period.

The determinants of the fair premium in this case will be the initial difference between, and the expected rates of growth of, assets and liabilities. The model is based on financial market equilibrium and thus produces the price that would occur in a competitive market with perfect information. In addition to deriving the guaranty fund premium equation, Cummins also provides rough numerical approximations of assessments based on reasonable assumptions on the risk and drift parameters in the model. The results of this exercise are encouraging, in that the estimated premiums are of reasonable orders of magnitude when compared with actual guaranty fund assessments in recent years.

Reliance on guaranty funds is clearly an option of last resort. Indeed, the fact that guaranty fund assessments have totaled less than $1 billion in the last 17 years suggests that insurers protect themselves reasonably adequately from insolvency.[15] Reinsurance is one of the primary means by which such protection is obtained. There are a wide number of different arrangements, but all involve a primary insurer ceding a portion of the insurance contract's risk to a secondary or assuming insurer. Typical arrangements include facultative contracts, in which the reinsurer assumes responsibility for losses on a specific risk, and treaty reinsurance, where the reinsurer pays a specified part of losses on all risks insured.

In pricing reinsurance, the traditional actuarial focus has been on the estimation of the loss severity distribution, in the case of individual excess contracts, or the aggregate loss distribution in the case of treaty reinsurance. These approaches can be computationally difficult, and often impose severe data requirements. In this volume, Doherty proposes an alternative methodology for pricing reinsurance, based on financial theory and options pricing models.

Doherty recognizes the essential similarity between a reinsurance contract and an option. An option offers the purchaser the opportunity to buy (a call option) or sell (a put option) a security at a fixed (striking) price on a given data (or over some given period). Such a contract has a payoff only if the security price on the expiration date exceeds (call) or falls short of (put) the striking price. An excess-of-loss reinsurance contact has similar features; it has a payoff if the losses on the primary policy exceed the threshold or deductible.

With this understanding, Doherty demonstrates that the options pricing models developed over the last decade can be applied directly to the reinsurance pricing problem. The benefits of this approach are predominantly the more modest data requirements and the arguably stronger theoretical foundations of models drawn from financial economics as opposed to actuarial theory.

Conclusions

The first half of this chapter briefly reviewed the current programs and procedures used to determine the market price of workers' compensation insurance. This pricing program has evolved over decades, as a continuing response to an ever changing environment. However, as the second half of the chapter indicates, concerns about equity and efficiency raise several important questions in regard to the determination of costs, the adjustment of prices, and the ability of the system to adequately fund its obligations.

Each chapter in this volume addresses at least one of these questions directly. As a whole, the volume represents the analyses and opinions of a group of scholars who are devoting their attention to one of the most important social insurance programs in the nation. While there are many questions that remain to be answered, their research immediately increases our understanding of workers' compensation pricing, suggests improvements to the current system, and provides direction for future work.

Notes

1 Although availability is technically not a problem due to the operation of assigned risk pools, the burgeoning growth of these residual market mechanisms has been a cause for concern in the last three years. In 1986, the National Workers' Compensation Reinsurance Pool became the largest writer of workers' compensation in the nation. Worrall, John D., ed. *Safety and the Work Force: Incentives and Disincentives in Workers' Compensation*. Ithaca, NY: ILR Press, 1983.

2 See *Safety and the Work Force: Incentives and Disincentives in Workers' Compensation* and Worrall, John D. and David Appel, eds. *Workers' Compensation Benefits: Adequacy, Equity, and Efficiency*. Ithaca, NY: ILR Press, 1985.

3 See Coase (1960) for a complete discussion.

4 This section is drawn from Lambrinos and Appel (1986). The classic treatise in the field is Kallop (1975), while a more complete explanation of workers' compensation insurance rate-making can be found in Webb et. al., (1984, Chapter 10, pp. 106–112 and 130–158) and various monographs available from the National Council on Compensation Insurance.

5 The classification codes are designed to identify different employments that may give rise to differential levels of injury risk. Thus, they are unlike the Standard Industrial Classification (SIC) codes, which are product, or output-based. Also, in several states there is a fourth industry group for oil-related activities.

6 The state minimums vary from $1250 to $3500 of annual premium.

7 The self-rating point varies by state from $600,000 to $2 million.

8 National Council on Compensation Insurance, "An In-Depth View of Experience Rating," 1982, page 10.

9 The exceptions are employers covered by the National Workers' Compensation Reinsurance Pool in states where discounts have been eliminated for assigned risks.

10 Choice of the plans is elective on the part of the insurer. In practice, many mutual companies elect the stock discount program.

11 "Casualty and Surety Rate Regulatory Bill," draft of May 18, 1946, as approved by the National Association of Insurance Commissioners, June 12, 1946, Section 3 (a) 4.

12 See National Commission on State Workmen's Compensation Laws (1972).

13 See, for example, Worrall and Appel (1982), Butler and Worrall (1983), and Dorsey

and Walzer (1983). See Worrall and Appel (1987) for a review of past research concerning benefit utilization.

14 In competitive markets, high-risk insurers would be forced to offer coverage at lower prices than low-risk insurers. Thus, insolvency risk would be priced efficiently. The presence of guaranty funds effectively renders all firms of equal risk, regardless of operating strategy.

15 This is a remarkably small sum when one considers that the industry's liabilities averaged well over $100 billion annually over this time period.

References

Berkowitz, Edward D., and Monroe Berkowitz. "Challenges to Workers' Compensation: An Historical Analysis." In John D. Worrall and David Appel (eds.), *Workers' Compensation Benefits: Adequacy, Equity, and Efficiency*. Ithaca, NY: ILR Press, 1985.

Butler, Richard J., and John D. Worrall. "Workers' Compensation: Benefit and Injury Claim Rates in the Seventies." *Review of Economics and Statistics*, November 1983: 580–589.

Coase, Ronald. "The Problem of Social Cost." *Journal of Law and Economics*, October 1960: 1–44.

Dorsey, Stuart, and Norman Walzer. "Workers' Compensation, Job Hazards, and Wages." *Industrial and Labor Relations Review*, July 1983: 642–654.

Kallop, Roy, "A Current Look at Workers' Compensation Ratemaking," *Proceedings of the Casualty Actuarial Society*, LXII, 1975, p. 62–133.

Lambrinos, James and David Appel, "Workers' Compensation and Employment: An Industry Analysis." In Monroe Berkowitz and M. Anne Hill (eds.), *Disability and the Labor Market*. Ithaca, NY: ILR Press, 1986.

National Commission on State Workmen's Compensation Laws. *The Report of the National Commission on State Workmen's Compensation Laws*. Washington, D.C.: Government Printing Office, 1972.

Ruser, John W. "Workers' Compensation Insurance, Experience Rating, and Occupational Injuries." *Rand Journal of Economics*, Winter 1983: 487–503.

Webb, Bernard L., J.J. Launie, Willis Park Rokes, and Norman A. Baglini. *Insurance Company Operations*. Third edition. Malvern, PA: American Institute for Property and Liability Underwriters, 1984.

Worrall, John D., and David Appel. "The Wage Replacement and Benefit Utilization in Workers' Compensation Insurance." *Journal of Risk and Insurance*, September 1982: 361–371.

Worrall, John D., and David Appel. "The Impact of Workers' Compensation Benefits on Low-Back Claims." In Nortin M. Hadler (ed.), *Clinical Concepts in Regional Musculoskeletal Illness*. Orlando, FL: Grune & Stratton, Inc., 1987.

2 LABOR MARKET THEORY AND THE DISTRIBUTION OF WORKERS' COMPENSATION LOSSES

Richard J. Butler
John D. Worrall

In recent years, a growing number of research papers have applied modern neoclassical labor economics to address incentive issues in the workers' compensation system. How these incentives can be detected in distributions of workers' compensation indemnity claims, and what they imply for those distributions, are the subjects of this research. We develop a simple statistical model that breaks down the observed distribution of indemnity payments into *choice, chance* and *heterogeneity* components, with particular attention given to how changes in the benefit structure (given market wage rates) and in experience rating affect claims. There is growing evidence (see our review in Worrall and Butler, 1985a) that the structure of benefits and experience rating may significantly change both the frequency with which claims are filed as well as the duration of a claim once it is

We wish to thank David Appel and Philip Borba for thoughtful discussions which stimulated this research, as well as for help in obtaining the data used in the analysis. The useful comments of anonymous referees considerably improved the present version of the paper. We are also grateful for computing support from the College of Family, Home and Social Sciences at Brigham Young University.

filed. Given the dynamic changes taking place in this enormous social insurance program, even small response effects have large distributional and efficiency impacts.

In the next section we develop simple alternative statistical models of the distribution of claims. For any given individual, we suggest that the distribution of time spent on a claim arising from chance will likely be quite different from a distribution that is the result of maximizing choice. However, whether that time on a claim for a given individual is a mostly choice or mostly chance event, we expect to see differences across individuals because of two sources of heterogeneity: *inherent* heterogeneity, which is the difference unrelated to measurable economic incentives, and *incentive* heterogeneity, which is the difference arising in firm and worker behavior because economic incentives change. We present estimates of these statistical models in the section on sample and estimation. Consistent with evidence reported elsewhere, we find that increases in benefits and decreases in wages or experience rating significantly increase the severity (i.e., the size) of claim losses. Some concluding observations are made in the last section.

Choice, Chance, and Heterogeneity in Indemnity Distributions

The Cost of a Claim

Workers' compensation benefits consist of virtually unlimited medical cost coverage associated with a workplace injury, as well as an indemnity benefit for workers whose injuries result in lost work time. In an earlier paper with David Appel (Butler, Worrall, and Appel, 1985), we analyzed the determinants of medical utilization under workers' compensation; in this paper we restrict ourselves to an analysis of indemnity payments. We use establishment data to examine the distribution of indemnity claims across firms, so we begin by modeling indemnity costs for the representative worker at a given firm. It is important to remember that the given-firm assumption will be used to generate a distribution of indemnity costs for a single subpopulation (i.e., those in that given firm), and these distributions may vary across firms because of inherent differences in tastes for risk (assuming such tastes are not functions of observable economic factors) or production technology associated with each specific firm. We will allow for this inherent heterogeneity below with mixing distributions, but first we need to develop the structural distribution that characterizes the distribution of costs for our subpopulation of workers (that is, for the representative worker at a given firm).

Since we will be looking at a cross section of firms at a point in time, we assume that the maximum level of indemnity payments (BENEFIT) and the level of experience rating (EXPRAT) are exogenously determined. The indemnity cost from the representative worker is simply the product of the benefit, the probability of filing a claim (PROB), and the duration of the claim (DURATION) once it has been filed. Since benefits and experience rating may affect either claims frequency or duration, the indemnity costs may be written as

$$\text{COST} = \text{BENEFIT} * \text{PROB(BENEFIT,EXPRAT)} \\ * \text{DURATION(BENEFIT,EXPRAT)}, \qquad (2.1)$$

where we suppresse wages in the PROB($\cdot$) and DURATION($\cdot$) functions for pedagogical reasons, but include them in the empirical specifications.

Chance and Choice

What are the stochastic processes which give rise to the distribution of costs for our given firm? It is well known that if PROB and DURATION are lognormally distributed, then (given the level of benefits) costs will also be distributed as a lognormal distribution. PROB or DURATION will in turn be distributed asymptotically as a lognormal if they represent the product of a sequence of independent, positive variates (any given claim is a product of such events: something breaks, someone happens to be standing nearby, the disposition to file a claim, the claim filing process, etc.) under some fairly mild restrictions.[1] This would be a pure chance generation of costs, with the level of benefits only affecting the distribution directly through the first right-hand term and not indirectly through the PROB and DURATION terms.

Against this chance (lognormal) distribution of indemnity costs, consider now an alternative model in which PROB and DURATION are treated jointly as the outcome of an employee maximization process in which the worker returns to work when his offered wage in the market exceeds his reservation wage (the minimum payment he will accept in order to return to work). Analogously to the treatment of unemployment insurance benefits,[2] an increase in benefits will increase the reservation wage and hence the observed durations of a claim, while higher employer costs (via experience rating) will tend to decrease duration and frequency of claims. In these (reservation wage) models, the resulting distribution of time on a claim (i.e., out of work) has nearly always been either a Weibull or exponential distribution (the latter being a special case of the former). Hence a simple choice distribution of indemnity costs will be assumed to be Weibull, the parameters of which will be a function of benefits, market wages, and experience rating.[3]

These two alternative distributions are given in the top of figure 2-1, along with their respective density functions. As shown there, both the lognormal (LN) and Weibull (W) are two-parameter distributions that turn out to be special cases of the three-parameter generalized gamma (GG) distribution. Hence if the indemnity claims from all firms were generated by the same choice or chance distribution, then we could check the importance of choice/chance by fitting W and LN distributions to the data and comparing them with the fit of the GG distribution, which includes both as special cases. This allows us to empirically determine the correct structural distribution.

Inherent Heterogeneity

Unfortunately it is well recognized that the structural distributions given in the top of figure 2-1 will vary across firms because of inherent differences (in management technique, production process, location, etc.) that generate different distributions of indemnity claims. To capture these differences, we assume that the form of structural distribution is the same for all firms except for the scale parameter, which will be assumed to follow an inverse generalized gamma distribution. If we denote the structural distribution by $f(y;\psi,\theta)$ and the mixing inverse generalized gamma distribution by IGG $(\theta;\phi)$, then the observed indemnity claims will be the average structural distribution, where the averaging occurs over the mixing distribution as follows:

$$h(y;\psi,\theta) = \int f(y;\psi,\theta)\mathrm{IGG}(\theta;\psi)d\theta. \tag{2.2}$$

The resulting observed distributions ($g(h;\psi,\theta)$) are given in the lower half of figure 2-1. They are the generalized beta of the second type (GB2), the logT (LT) and Burr type 12 (BR12, also known as the Singh–Maddala) distributions for the general, chance, and choice model distributions respectively. As is the case for the no-heterogeneity models, the observed distributions given heterogeneity (i.e., the LT and BR12 distributions) are special cases of the general GB2 distribution as indicated.

Tests for heterogeneity could simply be made by making comparisons of

Without Heterogeneity Across Subpopulations

General

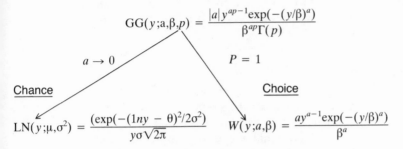

$$GG(y;a,\beta,p) = \frac{|a|\,y^{ap-1}\exp(-(y/\beta)^a)}{\beta^{ap}\Gamma(p)}$$

$a \to 0$ $P = 1$

Chance   Choice

$$LN(y;\mu,\sigma^2) = \frac{(\exp(-(1ny - \theta)^2/2\sigma^2)}{y\sigma\sqrt{2\pi}} \qquad W(y;a,\beta) = \frac{ay^{a-1}\exp(-(y/\beta)^a)}{\beta^a}$$

With Heterogeneity Across Subpopulations

$$GG \text{ } \theta \text{ } IGG = GB2$$
$$LN \text{ } \theta \text{ } IGG = LT$$
$$W \text{ } \theta \text{ } IGG = BR12$$

General

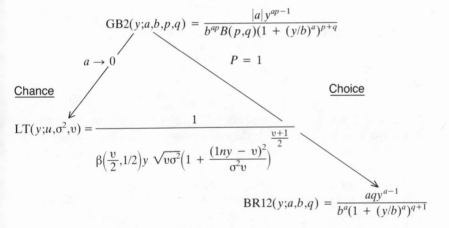

$$GB2(y;a,b,p,q) = \frac{|a|\,y^{ap-1}}{b^{ap}B(p,q)(1 + (y/b)^a)^{p+q}}$$

$a \to 0$ $P = 1$

Chance   Choice

$$LT(y;u,\sigma^2,\upsilon) = \frac{1}{\beta\left(\frac{\upsilon}{2},1/2\right)y\,\sqrt{\upsilon\sigma^2}\left(1 + \frac{(1ny - \upsilon)^2}{\sigma^2\upsilon}\right)^{\frac{\upsilon+1}{2}}}$$

$$BR12(y;a,b,q) = \frac{aqy^{a-1}}{b^a(1 + (y/b)^a)^{q+1}}$$

Note: The "IGG" distribution is simply the GG distribution with a negative value for the parameter "*a*".

Figure 2-1. Distribution of indemnity (*Y*) costs.

the relative distributional fit for the following: GB2 vs. GG, LT vs. LN, and BR12 vs. W. Tests between choice of models could be made on the basis of the following comparisons: GB2 vs. LT and GB2 vs. BR12. We present those tests in the section on sample and estimation, but first we look at heterogeneity across firms that is induced by economic incentives.

Incentive Differences

Not all differences in behavior across subpopulations of workers, and hence not all heterogeneity in the distribution of indemnity claims, is inherent. There is growing evidence that workers' claim frequencies and claim durations respond to the levels of benefits and wages, and that firms are sensitive to the degree of experience rating.[5] To allow for these incentive-induced differences, we made the scale parameter in our mixing distribution (the inverse generalized gamma function) a function of the levels of temporary total benefits, market wages, and the degree of experience rating. Given the theoretical and empirical results cited in footnote 5, our expectations are that the scale parameter of the mixing distribution (and hence the scale parameter of the observed distribution, and its implied mean as well—see figure 2-1) will increase with higher levels of benefits, and will decrease with higher market wages and more complete experience rating.

Hazard Rates

Aside from the form of the structural distribution implied by most reservation wage models (mainly, that the distribution be a Weibull), these models also imply that optimizing workers will leave claimant status at an increasing rate as the duration of the claim increases. That is, the conditional probability, or hazard rate, of leaving claimant status given that one has not yet left, is increasing with the duration of the claim. This auxiliary implication of the theory places restrictions on the form of the structural distribution which can be tested. An alternative view, which could be called the welfare dependency view, is that workers build up some claimant-specific capital[6] that makes leaving claimant status increasingly less attractive, decreasing the hazard rate. Hence tests of the welfare dependency view versus our choice model (the reservation wage view) hinges on whether the hazard rate is increasing or decreasing with the duration of a claim.

Sample and Estimation

The hypotheses discussed above will be sequentially examined in this section. Initially we will ignore induced heterogeneity (that is, differences in behavior resulting from changes in benefits, wages or experience rating) effects as we present evidence on the importance of heterogeneity in the distribution of claims. After we establish the importance of inherent heterogeneity, we then examine the empirical relevance of the choice and chance models of indemnity claims. Next we extend the model by allowing the scale parameter of the observed distribution to be a function of workers' compensation wages, benefits, and experience rating. The labor market theory hypotheses that we will be testing are as follows: that the reservation wage, or choice, model provides a superior fit to the data than the chance model (given the degree of inherent heterogeneity), so that either the W fits better than the LN (no inherent heterogeneity), or the BR12 fits better the LT distribution (inherent heterogeneity; see figure 2-1); and that induced heterogeneity operates as labor market theory predicts, that is, that indemnity losses will increase with higher levels of benefits and with lower levels of market wages and less complete experience rating. Finally, we test the additional implications of the choice model that the hazard rate of the distribution will be increasing as the duration of the claim increases.

Sample

The data used for the analysis was kindly provided to us by the National Council on Compensation Insurance, from their establishment data in the Risk Detail File. The data were reported for policy years 1980 and 1981. The losses have been evaluated as of the second report (18 months after the policy expiration). The data contain information for 38 states and for risks in 11 class codes. The 11 class codes (11 industries to be included in the analysis) were chosen on the basis of the extensive matching of NCCI codes and SIC codes that was done in Lambrinos and Appel (1985). See the data appendix for the list of industries included in the study and the sample mean statistics. The computer records included year (1980 or 1981), state, and class code identification as well as the indemnity losses, medical losses, total premium and payroll for each risk. The theory suggested by our discussion of equation (2.1) above considers losses per employee. Unfortunately, the number of employees per risk was not available in the data, although total payroll was. Hence, our analysis was restricted to an examination of indemnity losses per million dollars of payroll (instead of losses per worker).

Comparisons of Distributions

Table 2-1 summarizes our comparisons of alternative distributions of indemnity losses per million dollars of payroll (hereafter, simply "indemnity losses"). As explained below in connection with the discussion in figure 2-1, tests for the importance of inherent heterogeneity in our three alternative models (choice, chance, and the general model) is based on the comparisons listed in the upper three lines of table 2-1. The chi-square tests presented there are based on minus two times the difference in the value of the log-likelihood function for the distributions indicated. Significant differences in the fits of the distributions, namely those whose chi-square value exceeds the critical value (6.63 at the .01 level of significance), indicate that the hypothesis of no heterogeneity can be rejected. Although no heterogeneity in the model is soundly rejected in the general and choice models, it is not rejected in the chance model. That is, the LN distribution fits the data as well as LT distribution. However, to facilitate further comparisons, we assume that inherent heterogeneity is present in all models. In the context of our model, what this inherent heterogeneity implies is that even though individuals share a common structural distribution of claims *in form*, these distributions vary in their mean values because of *inherent* differences unrelated to our economic factors. As a result, the actual distribution of claims will have a fatter tail than would be expected under either a model of choice or of chance without the heterogeneity.

Testing for the best fit of the choice vs. chance models of claims is difficult because, even though both are special cases of the general model

Table 2-1. Comparing Alternative Distributions for Indemnity Data

Heterogeneity Tests		$\chi^2(1 \text{ d.f.})$
General Model	GB2 vs. GG	$\overline{0.27^*}$
Chance Model	LT vs. LN	0.0
Choice Model	BR12 vs. W	80.6*
Model Tests Given Heterogeneity		
General Model vs. Chance Model	GB2 vs. LT	14.2*
General Model vs. Choice Model	GB2 vs. BR12	23.7*

*Significant at the .01 level.

(GB2 when heterogeneity is present), the LT is a limiting form of the distribution. It is interesting that both the choice and chance models are rejected in favor of the more general model, with the chi-square value for the chance model being only half of that for the choice model in the comparisons. Again, since the LT is a limiting form of the GB2, no direct statistical tests are possible, although the smaller chi-square for the chance model suggests that, in some sense, it seems to fit somewhat better than the choice model. However, neither the choice nor the chance models fits the data as well as the GB2 (more general) distribution.

Incentive Heterogeneity

Since neither the choice nor chance models are clearly supported by the data, a more direct (and from a policy point of view, a more interesting) test of labor market effects on the distribution of losses can be made by seeing what effect benefits, wages, and experience rating have on the distribution of losses. To do this, we allow the scale parameter (b in the GB2 distribution of figure 2-1) to be a function of an intercept (a vector of ones), the maximum payment for temporary total benefits (TTMAX),[7] and average weekly industrial wages for production employees (WAGE). To capture the experience rating effect, we follow Ruser (1984) in estimating a benefit size interaction effect (TTMAX * SIZE is the product of TTMAX and millions of dollars of payroll). As discussed above in connection with footnote 5, we expect the estimated parameter of TTMAX * SIZE to be negative if experience rating is effective; that is, the benefit–frequency/duration effect should be smaller in larger (experience-rated) firms than smaller (manually rated) firms. To allow for different injury mixes across firms, we also included as a severity proxy the ratio of medical losses to all losses (SEV). We included all these effects in the GB2 maximum likelihood estimation with the following parameterization:

$$b = \exp(b1 + b2 * \text{TTMAX} + b3 * \text{WAGE}$$
$$+ b4 * (\text{TTMAX} * \text{SIZE}) + b5 * (\text{SEV})). \qquad (2.3)$$

Since the mean value of claims is proportional to the scale parameter b, under the labor market hypotheses referenced above we expect to observe the following pattern of signs: $b2 > 0$, $b3 < 0$, and $b4 < 0$.[8] To examine the robustness of the estimates, we tried alternative forms of the model as indicated in table 2-2. The implications in all these specifications is that the labor market theory finds some support. The models were all fit using MLE techniques with a 10^{-6} convergence criterion.

Table 2-2. Maximum Estimation of the General (GB2) Distribution (Absolute asymptotic t-statistics for slope parameters)

Parameter	Indemnity Payments Per $ Million Payroll			
	(1)	(2)	(3)	(4)
A	.3607	.3878	.3885	.3884
P	3.6145	3.5950	3.6059	3.6059
Q	5.7716	5.7680	5.7695	5.7695
CONST	9.4333	9.4189	9.4318	9.4318
TTMAX	.0041	.0041	.0053	.0054
	(2.83)	(2.96)	(3.37)	(3.71)
WAGE	−.0033	−.0045	−.0048	−.0047
	(1.83)	(2.63)	(2.77)	(2.78)
TTMAX*SIZE	—	−.5708E−9	—	−.0007
		(2.74)		(3.47)
SEV	—	—	−.001E−1	−.0003E−1
			(.00)	(.00)
$\mathscr{e}(E(Y)$, TTMAX$)$	.362	.362	.462	.469
$\mathscr{e}(E(Y)$, WAGE$)$	−.374	−.503	−.531	−.530
$\mathscr{e}(E(Y)$, TTMAX*SIZE$)$	—	−.572E−7	—	−.075
Implied Scale Parameter(b)	12,351	11,655	10,070	10,906
LNL	−14,359.8	−14,359.6	−14,359.1	−14,357.7

Note: All regressions contained 1425 observations. The MLE program was written in PROC MATRIX using the SAS computer package, with convergence criteria of 10^{-6}.

28

Since the coefficients are difficult to interpret by themselves, we have calculated the percent change in the average indemnity loss implied by a one-percent change in the respective incentive variables. We call these response effects *loss elasticities*, and present them after the estimated parameters in table 2-2. The elasticities of interest are of course the loss elasticities with respect to benefits and with respect to wages. Since our measure of the experience rating effect is necessarily an indirect one, this elasticity does not have the same direct interpretation that the other two have. Finally, we focus our discussion on specification 4 in table 2-2 although the results using the other specifications are obviously very similar.

There are several things to note about the benefit and wage loss elasticities. They are equal in magnitude, although opposite in sign, a result predicted by the simplest reservation wage and utility-maximizing theories.[9] Hence a one-percent increase in the benefits (decrease in the wages) implies about a one-half-percent increase in the expected losses. What does this mean? Returning to equation (2.1), suppressing the BENEFIT and EXPRAT arguments, we have

$$\text{COST} = \text{BENEFIT} * \text{PROB} * \text{DURATION}. \qquad (2.4)$$

The observed distribution of losses are given on the left-hand side, the product of the three terms on the right-hand side. Taking logarithms of both sides of equation (2.4) and differencing, we find that

$$\Delta\log(\text{COST}) = \Delta\log(\text{BENEFIT}) + \Delta\log(\text{PROB}) \\ + \Delta\log(\text{DURATION}). \qquad (2.5)$$

Now dividing through by the percentage change in benefits, we get

$$\frac{\Delta\log(\text{COST})}{\Delta\log(\text{BENEFIT})} = 1 + \frac{\Delta\log(\text{PROB})}{\Delta\log(\text{BENEFIT})} + \frac{\Delta\log(\text{DURATION})}{\Delta\log(\text{BENEFIT})}$$

$$= 1 + \mathscr{E}_{\text{P-B}} + \mathscr{E}_{\text{D-B}} \qquad (2.6)$$

where $\mathscr{E}_{\text{P-B}}$ and $\mathscr{E}_{\text{D-B}}$ are the benefit elasticities of the claims frequency and claims duration respectively. We would like to make inferences about the size of the sum of these two elasticities ($\mathscr{E}_{\text{P-B}} + \mathscr{E}_{\text{D-B}}$) on the right-hand side from the estimated elasticities given in table 2-2. Knowing these elasticities will greatly aid our ability to forecast the cost consequences of any further change in the structure of benefits.

However, because of data limitations, we could not directly estimate the elasticity on the left-hand side of equation (2.6), but rather—since indemnity costs per employee is indemnity costs per payroll divided by the wage—the following:

Table 2-3.   Hazard Rates for the Implied Structural Distribution $(GG(y;a,\theta,p))$ of Indemnity Claims: Model

Indemnity Payments per $ Million	Hazard Rates*			
	(1)	(2)	(3)	(4)
100	.0665	.0665	.0799	.0721
500	.0877	.1002	.1199	.1089
1,000	.0948	.1138	.1355	.1236
5,000	.0982	.1292	.1511	.1396
20,000	.0829	.1141	.1305	.1222
50,000	.0663	.0926	.1044	.0985
100,000	.0529	.0744	.0831	.0788

* Calculations based on the estimated coefficients given in Table 2. Hazard rates have all been multiplied by 10^4.

$$\frac{\Delta\log(\text{COST/WAGE})}{\Delta\log(\text{BENEFIT})} = \frac{\Delta\log(\text{COST})}{\Delta\log(\text{BENEFIT})} - \frac{\Delta\log(\text{WAGE})}{\Delta\log(\text{BENEFIT})}. \quad (2.7)$$

So whether we underestimated $(\mathscr{E}_{\text{P-B}} + \mathscr{E}_{\text{D-B}})$ or not depends on whether $\Delta\log(\text{WAGE})/\Delta\log(\text{BENEFIT})$ is greater than one or not. For example, if the wages increase in the face of constant maximum benefits (which are in fact less than the average wage), then the percentage change in wages will exceed the percentage change in benefits, and the estimated left-hand elasticity in equation (2.7) will exceed the sum of the two right-hand elasticities in equation (2.6). In this case, .469 would be a lower bound on those two elasticities. If the maximum benefits increase and wages are constant, then $\Delta\log(\text{WAGE})/\Delta\log(\text{BENEFIT})$ is less than one and .469 would be a upper bound. In the presence of increasing real wages and increasing maximums, the bias is indeterminate. However, given that the average wage exceeds the maximum and changes in the maximums are often tied to average wages, it is not unlikely that the bias will be small.

How does the .469 square with extant elasticities of $\mathscr{E}_{\text{P-B}}$ and $\mathscr{E}_{\text{D-B}}$? Elsewhere, we (Worrall and Butler, 1985) review estimates from several studies, all using techniques and data considerably different from those employed here. We find estimates in the literature of around .4 for the claims elasticity, $\mathscr{E}_{\text{P-B}}$, and from .1 to .4 for the duration elasticity, $\mathscr{E}_{\text{D-B}}$. Our paper—using a considerably more sophisticated stochastic structure than previous researchers—confirms the size and importance of these elasticities. The evidence indicates that a 10 percent increase in benefits will increase costs by 15 per cent $((1 + .469) * .10$, using equation (2.6)).

Finally, table 2-3 presents the hazard rates for each of the four implied structural distributions in table 2-2. The hazard rate is evaluated at the mean levels of the independent variables, allowing the size of the losses to increase. In each case, the hazard rate is an increasing function of the size of the claim up to about the mean level of indemnity losses. This is consistent with many reservation wage models (some other reservation wage models predict a constant hazard rate). However, after this level hazard rates begin to decline, suggesting that the welfare dependence effects (or other stochastic processes) may be dominating the observed distribution at the higher loss levels.

Conclusions

Since the publication of the *Report of the National Commission on State Workmen's Compensation Laws* in 1972, many states have adopted the Commission's recommendations that there be substantial increases in the benefit levels of the workers' compensation system. While these have helped to alleviate concerns about the adequacy of work-related injury benefits, our estimates—and those of others referenced here and elsewhere—consistently point to substantial incentive effects. In particular, increases in the benefits (as well as decreases in the market wage rate) have not only a direct one-to-one effect on costs, but also increase costs indirectly through the incentive effects that benefits have on claims frequency and claims duration. Using very different techniques (i.e., fitting a parameterized GB2 function by MLE methods), we find elasticities remarkably similar to those already in the literature. Hopefully, not only will the models and estimation techniques presented here be useful to future researchers in this area, but also the conclusions will help guide policy makers in this interesting period of dynamic changes in the program structure.

Notes

1 See respectively theorems 2.2 and 2.9 in Atchison and Brown (1969). If the means or variance of the generating variables in theorem 2.9 are determined by the level of benefits (or experience rating), then the independence of the distributions breaks down and theorem 2.9 no longer applies.

2 See various articles in the special 1985 issue of *Journal of Econometrics* edited by Kiefer and references cited there.

3 Employer incentives under experience rating affect the employee's behavior in an implicit contract in which employees benefit/duration response varies with the preparation of workers' compensation costs borne directly by the firm. In particular, as we have discussed

elsewhere (1985), larger firms usually bear 100 percent of their workers' compensation costs (i.e., they are perfectly experience-rated), and so have stronger incentives to encourage employees not to increase their claims frequency or duration in the face of higher benefits. Hence, the employee benefit response should be lower in larger firms.

4 An inverse generalized gamma is a generalized gamma distribution with shape parameter being negative. For a more general treatment on mixing distributions, see McDonald and Butler (1985).

5 Increases in claims frequency with respect to higher benefits/lower wages are found in Butler (1983), Butler and Worrall (1983), Chelius (1973, 1974, 1977, 1982, 1983), Ruser (1984), and Worrall and Appel (1982). Claim duration effects with respect to the same variables are reported in Butler and Worrall (1985), Worrall, Butler, Borba and Durbin (1985), and Worrall and Butler (1985c). Experience rating effects (i.e., experience-rated firms have lower claims rate/durations, *ceterus paribus*) are reported in Ruser (1984) and Worrall and Butler (1985a), while Chelius and Smith find no experience rating effects (1983).

6 The idea is a simple one: the longer one is a claimant, the more one understands claimant status (institutions) and the more one's knowledge about the work force depreciates. Hence, in a relative sense, it becomes increasingly difficult to leave claimant status and return to work. See Stigler and Becker (1977) for a generalization of these ideas.

For a more detailed discussion of the hazard rate in the context of the workers' compensation system, see Worrall and Butler (1985c).

7 We would have preferred to use the expected benefit given the wage distribution, since this would have incorporated the effect of the replacement ratio and minimum payments as well as the maximum. However, wage data by state *and* industry were not available, so rather than use industry-wide wages and potentially introduce errors in the variable bias into our measured benefit effect, we chose rather just to use the maximum payment for temporary total claims. Most claims are temporary total, and the maximum payment for permanent partial injuries (the next most common claimant status) is highly correlated with the temporary total claims.

8 The expected mean of the GB2 is $b B\left(p + \dfrac{1}{a}, q - \dfrac{1}{a}\right)/B(p, q)$. Upon substituting from equation (2, 3) and taking logarithms on both sides, we see that

$$\ln E(Y) = \ln(\exp(Xb)) + \ln(\text{Constant}),$$

so that

$$\frac{\delta \ln E(Y)}{\delta \ln Xi} = X_i b_i.$$

9 Similar empirical results were obtained in Butler and Worrall (1985).

References

Aitchison, J., and J.A.C. Brown *The Lognormal Distribution: With Special Reference to its Uses in Economics*. Cambridge: Cambridge University Press, 1969.

Butler, Richard J., and John D. Worrall. "Workers' Compensation: Benefit and Injury Claim Rates in the Seventies." *Review of Economics and Statistics* 4 November 1983: 580–589.

Butler, Richard J. "Wage and Injury Rate Response to Shifting Levels of Workers' Compensation." In John D. Worrall (ed.), *Safety and the Work Force: Incentives and Disincentives in Workers' Compensation*. Ithaca, NY: ILR Press, 1983.

Bulter, Richard J., and John D. Worrall. "Work Injury Compensation and the Duration of Nonwork Spells." *Economic Journal*, September 1985: 714–724.

Chelius, James R. "Workers' Compensation and the Incentive to Prevent Injuries." In John D. Worrall (ed.), *Safety and the Work Force: Incentives and Disincentives in Workers' Compensation*. Ithaca, NY: ILR Press, 1983.

Chelius, James R. "The Influence of Workers' Compensation on Safety Incentive." *Industrial and Labor Relations Review* January 1982: 235–242.

Chelius, James R. *Workplace Safety and Health*. Washington, DC: American Enterprise Institute, 1977.

Cheilus, James R. "The Control of Industrial Accidents: Economic Theory and Empirical Evidence." *Law and Contemporary Problems*, Summer/Autumn 1974: 700–729.

Chelius, James R. "An Empirical Analysis of Safety Regulation." In Vol. 3, *Supplemental Studies for the National Commission on State Workmen's Compensation Laws*. Washington, DC: U.S. Government Printing Office, 1973.

Chelius, James R., and Robert S. Smith. "Experience Rating and Injury Prevention." In John D. Worrall (ed.), *Safety and the Work Force: Incentives and Disincentives in Workers' Compensation*. Ithaca, NY: ILR Press, 1983.

Johnson, William, G. "Work Disincentives of Benefit Payments." In John D. Worrall (ed.), *Safety and the Work Force: Incentives and Disincentives in Workers' Compensation*. Ithaca, NY: ILR Press, 1983.

Kiefer, Nicholas (ed.). "Duration Models in Economics." Special issue of the *Journal of Econometrics* 28 (1985).

Lambrinos, James, and David Appel, "Workers' Compensation and Employment: An Industry Analysis," In Monroe Berkowitz and Anne Hill (eds.), *Disability and the Labor Market*. Ithaca, NY: ILR Press, 1986.

McDonald, James B., and Richard J. Butler, "Some Generalized Mixture Distributions," *Review of Economics and Statistics*, May 1987: 232–240.

Ruser, John W. "Workers' Compensation Insurance, Experience Rating and Occupational Injuries," *Rand Journal of Economics*, 16, (1985): 487–503.

Stigler, George I., and Gary S. Becker. "De Gustibus Non Est Disputandum." *American Economic Review*, January 1977: 76–90.

Worrall, John D., and David Appel. "Some Benefit Issues in Workers' Compensation." In John D. Worrall and David Appel (eds.), *Benefit Issues in Workers' Compensation: Adequacy, Equity and Efficiency*. Ithaca, NY: ILR Press, 1985.

Worrall, John D., and David Appel. "The Wage Replacement Rate and Benefit Utilization in Workers' Compensation Insurance." *Journal of Risk and Insurance* 49, 3 (1982): 361–371.

Worrall, John D., David Appel and Richard J. Butler, "Sex, Marital Status, and Medical Utilization by Injured Workers," *Journal of Risk and Insurance*, March 1987: 27–44.

Worrall, John D., and Richard J. Butler. "Experience Rating Matters." Paper presented at NCCI Conference, *Economic Issues in Workers' Compensation*, 1985a.

Worrall, John D., and Richard J. Butler, "Some Lessons of Workers' Compensation," In Monroe Berkowitz and Anne Hill (eds.), *Disability and the Labor Market*. Ithaca, NY: ILR Press, 1986.

Worrall, John D., and Richard J. Butler. "Workers' Compensation: Benefits and Duration of Claims." In John D. Worrall and David Appel (eds.), *Benefit Issues in Workers' Compensation: Adequacy, Equity and Efficiency*. Ithaca, NY: ILR Press, 1985c.

Worrall, John D., Richard J. Butler, Philips Borba, and David Durbin, "Estimating the Exit Rate from Workers' Compensation: New Hazard Rate Estimates," March 1988, mimeo.

Worrall, John D. "Compensation Costs, Injury Rates and the Labor Market." In John D. Worrall (ed.), *Safety and the Labor Force: Incentives and Disincentives in Workers' Compensation*. Ithaca, NY: ILR Press, 1983.

Data Appendix

Source: See text (computer files from NCCI).
Date: All data in real 1967 dollars.

Variable	Means	Standard Deviation
COSTS	14,900.6	48,647.2
WAGE	111.78	27.99
TTMAX	87.24	35.83
TTMAX*SIZE	100.25	228.99
SEV	.527	.235

Industries in the sample (NCCI code, SIC): Shoe (2260, 314), Furniture (2883, 2511), Tires (4420, 301), Alcohol (2130, 2082), Jewelry (3383, 3911), Stationary (4251, 2642), Printing (4299, 2752), Musical instruments (2923, 393), Automobile (3808, 3711), Oil and Gas (4740), 291).

States in the Sample: AL, AK, AZ, ARK, CO, CT, DC, FL, GA, ID, IL, IN, IA, KS, KY, LA, ME, MD, MS, MO, MT, NE, NH, NM, OK, OR, RI, SC, SD, TN, UT, VT, HI.

WAGE data: Earnings and Employment, 1984 Supplementary, U.S. Dept. of Labor.

BENEFIT data: State Compliance with the 19 Essential Recommendations of the National Commission On State Workmen's Compensation Laws, 1972–1980, U.S. Dept. of Labor, January 1981 and *Monthly Labor Review*, March 1982.

3 DISABILITY RELATED CATEGORIES: AN ALTERNATIVE TO WAGE LOSS BENEFITS FOR INJURED WORKERS

James Lambrinos, Ph.D.
William G. Johnson, Ph.D.

This chapter describes a prospective payment system for workers' compensation benefits, modeled on the DRG system which is used for paying hospitals.

The wage-loss method of benefit determination is quite common for workers' compensation (WC) temporary total disability claims. Workers are typically paid two-thirds of their weekly wage, within certain limits, for the length of their absence from work. This type of system is retrospective in the sense that the benefits depend upon absence from work. An inefficiency is created because retrospective benefits provide a disincentive to return to work not unlike cost-based reimbursement to hospitals producing incentives for excessive use of health care services. In this chapter, we survey the literature on the disincentives of workers' compensation benefits and propose a prospective method of benefit determination based upon a classification system called Disability-Related Categories (DRCs).

The authors would like to thank, without implication, David Appel, John Burton, Jr., and an anonymous referee for their useful comments and suggestions.

The prospective payment system has revolutionized the method of reimbursing hospitals for Medicare patients. Central to the payment system is a classification system called diagnosis-related groups (DRGs) which places patients in categories that are relatively homogeneous in terms of resource use. The appeal of such a classification system is relatively straightforward. DRGs create an incentive to minimize the cost of a hospital visit by providing the hospital with a fixed payment upon admission. Hospitals that provide care at costs lower than the fixed payment keep the excess revenues. Similarly, hospitals lose money on patients for whom the costs of treatment are greater than the prospective payment.

A prospective payment system is used in New York State to determine Medicaid's payments to long-term care facilities and soon will be extended to payments for outpatient services. Capitation payments to health maintenance organizations by Medicare and Medicaid are also prospective. Prospective payments will probably become more common as pressures for containing health care costs increase.

In this chapter, we begin by discussing some of the disincentive effects created by the current workers' compensation system. We suggest that the disincentive effects of the current system can be reduced through the use of a prospective payment system. The proposed payment system would be used to determine indemnity benefits and is not intended to be used as a medical fee schedule. Since the method of classification is similar to the one used to develop DRGs, we next examine the methods used to create the DRG categories, briefly review how DRGs are being used as a reimbursement mechanism, and describe how the DRG methodology can be adapted to produce Disability-Related Categories. Rather than decomposing variations in length of hospital stays, the DRC method decomposes variations in work-loss days associated with different illnesses or injuries. We then describe a model which can be used to develop the DRCs.

In the next section, we discuss a method of applying the DRC concept to workers' compensation and the final section contains a brief summary and some conclusions.

The Disincentive Effects of Workers' Compensation Benefits

Since disincentive effects of workers' compensation benefits may fluctuate with the type of benefit as well as the type of claim, this section has been divided into three parts: temporary disability, permanent partial disability, and wage-loss benefits. In addition to a discussion of the literature concerning the disincentive effects for these categories, a brief review of studies dealing with equity and adequacy will be included.

Temporary Disability

Temporary total disability is the most common type of workers' compensation claim. Temporary claims are typically of short duration and the average benefit is low. The average benefit in New York State, for example, was $1107 in 1982, and total payments for temporary disability benefits were only 15 percent of workers' compensation benefits in 1982. The DRC approach could reduce expenditures on temporary disability claims by improving incentives to return to work and by reducing administrative expenses.

The work disincentives of temporary disability benefits probably exceed those from permanent disability benefits because workers with temporary disabilities bear a lower proportion of the costs of absence from work. Some of the reasons for the difference are (1) workers do not lose seniority rights or eligibility for fringe benefits because of short absences from work; (2) employers have less incentive to replace a worker with a short-term disability; (3) the absolute wage losses from most short-term disabilities are too low to significantly reduce a worker's assets; (4) the real value of WC benefits declines over time because they have not been adjusted for inflation (the longer the duration of benefits, the lower the real replacement ratio); (5) benefits are paid only if the worker is absent from his or her job; and (6) the average expenditure on temporary claims is too low to justify the medical and vocational evaluations needed to eliminate moral hazard.

These facts suggest that substantial savings could be obtained by using DRCs to calculate benefit payments for temporary total disability. Speculations about potential savings are, however, poor substitutes for empirical estimates. Unfortunately, there are only three studies of the disincentive effects of temporary disability benefits, and their results are contradictory.

Chelius (1982) finds that the number of days lost per case is negatively related to the ratio of WC benefits to wages. The elasticity of days lost per case to the replacement ratio is $-.09$.[1] The data are for 36 states for the years 1972–1975. Benefits are measured as the statutory (not the actual) benefits for temporary total injuries in each state. The wage variable is the average weekly wages (by industry) in each state in each of the three years.

Curington (1983) extends Chelius's study, using data for 13 years (1964–1976) from New York State and adding controls for firm size and business cycle variations in employment and work hours. No significant relationship is found between workers' compensation benefits and the number of lost workdays. When the data are separated into temporary total and permanent disability cases, benefits do not affect lost workdays for temporary disability, but lost days among permanently disabled workers are positively related to benefit levels.

The Chelius and Curington results are constrained by their reliance on aggregate data. The wage variable is average wages for all workers in a state and benefits equal statutory maxima. Butler and Worrall used microdata to study workers' compensation benefits and the duration of claims. The data are from an NCCI survey of closed cases for temporary disability claims for low back conditions in the state of Illinois. They find that the duration of a claim increases from two to four percent with a 10 percent increase in the ratio of benefits to wages and that total expenditures by the WC plan increase by 12–14 percent with the 10 percent increase in benefits.

Butler and Worrall's results are perhaps the most reliable because they use data on individual workers and actual benefits rather than statutory maxima. The disincentive effects of benefits paid for low back claims are, however, likely to be different from those for other temporary total claims. Impairments of the lower back are chronic conditions rather than the acute, one-time injuries that typify most temporary disability claims. The well-known difficulty of separating true claims for low back conditions from counterfeits suggests that the disincentives measured by Butler and Worrall are larger than those among other temporary disability beneficiaries.

Even if the true elasticities are small, stronger work incentives could produce large savings because the number of temporary disability claims is large. In New York State, for example, 71,375 workers received slightly more than $79 million in temporary disability benefits in 1982.

Much of the costs of administering temporary disability claims are fixed by the procedural requirements of workers' compensation laws. Since average benefits are small ($1100 in New York State), the costs of administration are likely to be a relatively high proportion of benefits. A prospective method of payment, such as the DRCs, reduces administrative expenses by calculating benefits from information collected at the time of injury. We do not know how much might be saved per case, but potential savings are large because of the large number of temporary disability claims.

Ideally, DRCs would eliminate only the benefits paid for voluntary absences from work. The chances that DRCs approach this ideal depend on the accuracy with which the method predicts the number of days of involuntary absences from work. If the prediction error is small, payments will be distributed equitably. Information on the adequacy and equity of current temporary disability payments is required for even a speculative discussion of the impact of DRCs. The information that is available is old and limited to two states.

Jarvis used hypothetical cases and the provisions of the Washington WC law to evaluate the adequacy of temporary total disability benefits in 1971. He defined *adequate* as a ratio of benefits to losses that exceeds 66⅔ percent. He found that

1. Workers with low wages, particularly those with larger families, may be reimbursed for more than 100 percent of their lost income;
2. Single workers bear a burden of lost income which is as much as twice the amount borne by workers who earn the same gross pay but have a wife and five children.

Jolivette (1969) studied Wisconsin workers' compensation benefits for temporary disability. He concludes that benefits are inadequate because of benefit maxima and a mandatory waiting period before benefits are paid. Some of his data, however, contradict his assertions. They show, for example, that a worker with no dependents who earned the 1969 Wisconsin maximum wage would receive weekly benefits equal to 90 percent of his after-tax wage income (p. 967, table 3).

A more current and comprehensive analysis of temporary disability benefits is needed. We suspect that such an analysis would show temporary disability benefits to be more adequate than benefits for permanent disability.[2] If for no other reason, this result should occur because price inflation erodes the adequacy of benefits for claims of longer duration.

The Jarvis study suggests that overcompensation for temporary disability is common among low-income workers. Jolivette's replacement ratios for higher-income workers exceed the standard of 66⅔ percent of the predisability wage. Since both Jarvis and Jolivette measure wage losses without controlling for the work disincentives of benefits, it is possible that DRCs can reduce moral hazard without significantly reducing the adequacy of benefits, providing a more equitable distribution of temporary disability benefits.

Temporary injuries are the most prevalent type of workers' compensation claim. Injuries that cause permanent partial disabilities are less frequent but more expensive. The use of DRCs to determine benefits for permanent partial disability is the subject of the next section.

Permanent Partial Disability

In most workers' compensation jurisdictions, scheduled benefits are the usual method of compensation for permanent partial impairments. Scheduled benefits are fixed amounts based on the type and severity of the worker's impairment. Circumstances such as age or skill that cause wage losses to vary among similarly impaired workers are not considered in fixing the benefit amounts, nor do benefits vary with the worker's duration of absence from work.

The original workers' compensation laws calculated benefits according to wage losses. Scheduled benefits were introduced to reduce litigation regarding the effect of an injury on a person's ability to work (Larson, 1980, p. 508). Only major impairments, such as the loss of an arm, eye, hand or foot were scheduled. It was presumed that major impairments caused a wage loss in every case.

These simple and probably realistic assumptions have been replaced by schedules that vary so much among states that it is impossible to describe them in terms of a unifying principle. Contemporary schedules, instead of reducing litigation, create much of the litigation about workers' compensation claims. Ironically, the inequity of scheduled benefits has led many workers' compensation plans to "introduce" wage-loss benefits for permanent partial disability (Weiler, 1983). Many of the inequalities are caused by the failure to adequately distinguish between long- and short-term work disability created by permanent partial impairments. The problem originates from the uncertainty concerning the effect of a physical impairment on a person's ability to work. An extensive literature demonstrates that the type and severity of impairment is a poor predictor of whether an impaired person works or withdraws from the labor force (Berkowitz and Johnson, 1974; Parsons, 1977; Yelin, Nevit, and Epstein, 1980; Chirikos and Nestel, 1984). Better predictions are obtained if influences such as the physical demands of the person's usual job, economic incentives for work, and employer discrimination are also considered.

California adjusted its schedules to reflect the influence of age and occupation on the work capacity of impaired workers, but scheduled benefits in California are not equitably distributed (CWCI, 1985). The failure of most benefit schedules is caused by the shortage of information on the determinants of wage losses and work absences among partially impaired workers. Lacking objective data, most states set scheduled benefits according to opinions based on a very partial understanding of the facts.

The complexity of the relationship between permanent partial impairments and work-loss days is demonstrated by the results presented in table 3-1. The equation, which estimated data of workers who received scheduled benefits in New York State, includes age, industry, occupation, sex and the severity and nature of injury, but accounts for only 22 percent of the variation in work-loss days among injured workers (Johnson and Curington, 1986). The difficulties of measuring these relationships make it obvious

Table 3-1. Duration of Absence from Work among Workers with Permanent Partial Disabilities Estimated as a Function of the Workers' Characteristics (duration expressed in years)

Variable	Coefficient	t ratio
Intercept	0.503	1.00
Demographics		
Age	0.004	0.78
Age 46–60	0.224	1.71*
Sex	−0.165	−1.00
Severity of impairment	0.048	7.70*
Occupation[a]		
Professional and managerial	−0.652	−2.66*
Clerical and sales	0.265	1.12
Service	0.041	0.19
Skilled	−0.421	−2.89*
Labor	0.071	0.42
Industry[b]		
Agriculture	0.963	1.98*
Construction	0.682	2.03*
Manufacture of nondurables	0.082	0.25
Manufacture of durables	−0.044	−0.14
Transportation	0.071	0.20
Wholesale trade	0.195	0.50
Retail trade	0.183	0.54
Finance, insurance, and real estate	−0.508	−1.13
Service	0.210	0.61
Government	0.231	0.53
Nature of Injury[c]		
Bruises, contusions, poisons	−0.875	−3.03*
Sprains, dislocations, fractures	−1.040	−2.41*
Amputations	−1.040	−3.41*
Burns	−0.022	−0.05
Hernias	3.642	2.94*
Hearing loss	−0.314	−0.34
Depuytren's contracture	−1.002	−1.51

R Square = .220*
N = 528   Mean Duration = 0.807

[a] The reference category is "Semi-Skilled."
[b] The reference categories are "Mining" and "Public Utilities."
[c] The reference category is "Not Elsewhere Classified."
* This value is significant at the 95 percent level of confidence or better.
Source: Johnson and Curington (1986), p. 21.

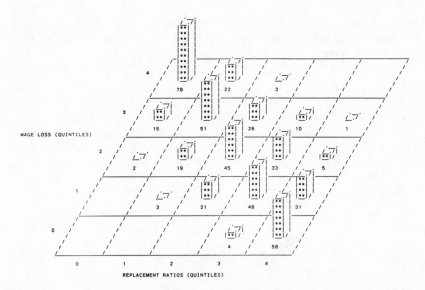

Figure 3-1. Workers who received scheduled benefits for permanent partial disability in New York State: wage loss vs. replacement ratios (cell totals = number of cases).

Source: Johnson and Curington (1986), p.37.

that ad hoc estimates of the influence of impairment on work losses are poor predictors of injured workers' wage losses.

Hope for a scientific calculation of scheduled benefits is also limited by the political process through which workers' compensation laws are amended. Schedules are frequently created by compromises among insurers, organized labor, and management. Political compromises based on poor information produce schedules that overcompensate minor impairments and undercompensate workers with serious work disabilities. Figure 3-1 illustrates how the adequacy of scheduled benefits, as reflected by the replacement ratio, declines as the size of wage losses increases. The perverse relationship between scheduled benefits and wage losses was described as early as 1916 by P. Tecumseh Sherman, who concluded that "the compensation fixed in such schedules for the minor injuries is sometimes fairly generous, that allowed for the major injuries is absurdly insufficient" (Sherman, 1916).

Research on scheduled benefits suggests that disincentives to return to work are minimized for those least able to work and maximized for those able to return to work soon after injury. Unfortunately, no one has estimated the disincentive effects of scheduled benefits from data that separate beneficiaries by their ability to work. Johnson's study of New York beneficiaries estimates the elasticity of labor force participation relative to workers' compensation benefits to be −0.088. This result is, however, estimated from a cohort in which 7.4 percent of the workers never return to work in the five years following injury. Since it is likely that the workers who never go back to work are physically unable to work, the true disincentives of scheduled benefits are probably greater than these results indicate.[3] Most of the current concern with scheduled benefits is with the inequity of compensation rather than with disincentives to work. Another study of scheduled benefits in New York State suggests that improvements in equity might be accomplished without substantially increasing expenditures.[4] The workers lost $5,048,024 in foregone gross wages and received $3,351,381 in scheduled benefits.[5] Sixty-two and three-tenths percent of the total wage loss was incurred by 39 workers who did not return to work after their accidents. The 39 workers received $375,229 in benefits, replacing an average of 11.9 percent of their losses. Benefits totaling $176,108 were paid to 44 other workers with no wage losses and the balance ($2,800,044) went to 443 workers whose wage losses totaled $1,887,409. If each worker had been paid 66⅔ percent of gross wage loss, total benefit payments would have increased by only 0.9 percent.

We have described the fundamental problem of evaluating the effects of a permanent partial impairment in work and wages. The nature of the problem suggests that more adequate information on postinjury work is a first step toward a more equitable distribution of workers' compensation benefits.

Many states are considering wage-loss benefits as a replacement for permanent partial benefit schedules. In the next section we consider some of the problems of achieving the goals of wage-loss benefits.

Wage-Loss Benefits

Some states and several Canadian provinces pay wage-loss benefits for a permanent partial disability. The benefits characteristically combine a scheduled benefit with additional payments to workers who sustain wage losses. Few U.S. states have true wage-loss benefit plans. New York is one of the exceptions, paying wage-loss benefits (*nonscheduled benefits* is the New York State terminology) for selected impairments, among which low back problems are the most common. Wage-loss benefits are quite costly. In New York State, for example, nonscheduled benefits were paid to only

4.2 percent of its cases, but the payments were 52.4 percent of benefits paid to all cases in 1982 (NYSWCB, 1982, p. 18).

A successful wage-loss system would be more equitable than are scheduled benefits. The success of wage-loss benefit plans depends, as does the equity of scheduled benefits, on the workers' compensation agency's ability to distinguish voluntary from involuntary work absences. The complexity of the problem is illustrated by the provisions of the Florida law governing wage-loss benefits (Berkowitz and Burton, 1983). The law requires that the following conditions be satisfied:

1. The worker must incur at least a 15 percent loss of earnings;
2. Benefits equal 95 percent of the (85 percent) earnings loss;
3. Benefits cannot exceed 66⅔ percent of the preinjury wage of 100 percent of the average weekly wage in Florida;
4. Benefits end at age 65. SSA early retirement benefits are offset against the WC payments;
5. Wage loss is defined relative to the wages that the injured worker is "able" to earn.

There are other conditions, but this list is sufficient to show the problem. It is obvious, for example, that the definition of what an injured worker is able to earn is subject to great uncertainty. The DRC alternative does not solve this problem but offers a method of imposing limits on wage-loss benefits that relies more on experience than on prior judgments.

Legislators should and will be suspicious of payment systems, such as DRCs, that rely on average rather than individual worker's wages and work. The DRC system does not exclude legislative judgements. It does provide a more objective basis for making those judgements.

In the next section we describe the concepts, methods and data used to create DRCs.

Methods for Creating DRCs

Since the proposed Disability-Related Categories mirror the techniques used to create DRGs, review of the development and application of the DRGs will be useful.

Diagnosis-Related Groups

The classification of patients into DRGs was originated by the Yale University School of Management and Organization (Fetter et al., 1980). The

DRGs were first applied to utilization review and quality assurance rather than the calculation of payments to providers.

The variables used to obtain the DRGs were age, sex, presence or absence of surgical procedure, and clinical complications. The current DRGs are based on 400,000 of 1.4 million records from acute care hospitals in the third and fourth quarters of 1979 and 335,000 records from New Jersey where the original DRGs were used as a reimbursement mechanism.

The DRG classification system seeks to group acute-care patients by similarities in resource consumption. The dependent variable is length of stay (LOS). LOS is a useful measure of resource use because it is readily available, it is uniform across hospitals, and it reflects variations in resources used among hospital patients, since length of stay is a major determinant of resource consumption. The disadvantage of the LOS measure is that it does not capture all the variation in resource consumption. Patients with the same length of stay often consume vastly different quantities of resources.

The variation in LOS is partitioned among a set of variables that influence resource consumption. The variables include presence of an operating room procedure, principal diagnosis, age, sex, the presence of a complication or comorbidity, and discharge status.

The first step in the construction of the DRGs is to assign patients to one of 23 Major Diagnostic Categories (MDCs) which correspond roughly to major body organ systems, such as Heart Disease or Diseases of the Liver. The next step is to identify independent variables which further reduce the variation in length of stay. Physician judgments are combined with a statistical algorithm to determine the independent variables that partitioned the patients into homogeneous groups. An interactive system called AUTOGRP was used as the statistical algorithm to develop the original DRGs.

The current DRG system contains 470 categories. Figure 3-2 describes the decomposition of all urinary calculus patients into the initial DRGs #239–242, using presence and type of surgery and presence of a secondary diagnosis as partitioning variables.

Several additional steps are necessary to convert this classification system into a workable payment system. First, the relevant costs must be defined and estimated for each DRG. The costs have been defined to be all inpatient operating costs which include routine services, ancillary and special care services, and malpractice costs.

The costs per DRG are averaged to arrive at a standardized amount. Initially, this amount was primarily based on the hospital's costs. It will gradually shift toward an amount based upon regional costs and, ultimately, toward national costs. The DRG relative weight reflects the cost of each specific DRG relative to the standardized amount.

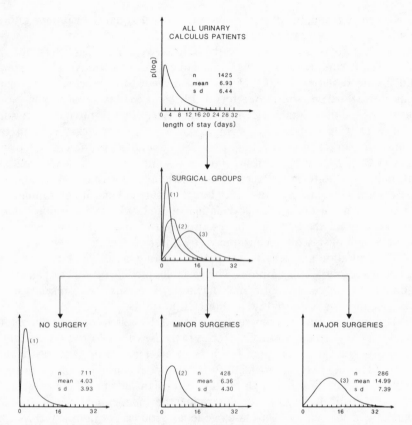

Figure 3-2. Decomposition of urinary calculus patients. Reprinted from Fetter et al., *Medical Care* (1980), with permission from J.B. Lippincott Company.

For example, if the standardized amount is $3300 then a fracture of the femur carries a payment of $5743 since it contains a relative weight of 1.7403.

Several additional adjustments are made to arrive at the final payment. If the standardized amount is expressed in 1982 dollars, then it must be inflated to the year in which it is being applied for reimbursement purposes. In addition, the standardized amount must also be adjusted to reflect differences in the costs of employment by a wage index. The impact of a teaching program on costs is incorporated by an index which reflects the number of residents and interns per hospital bed. Finally, payments need to be adjusted for variations in case-mix among hospitals to represent the increased costs of treating older, more severely ill patients.

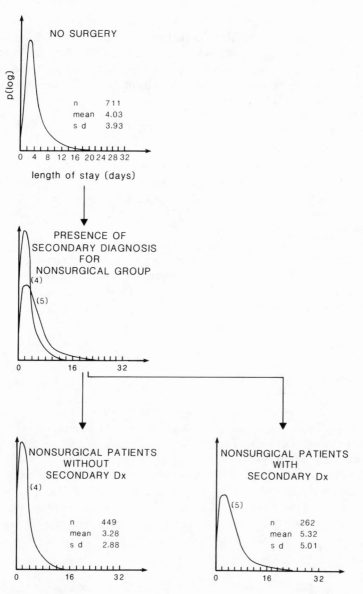

Figure 3-2. cont'd.

The DRG system has been criticized because considerable variation in resource use exists within the DRG categories. This variation appears to be related to the severity of the illness rather than to the type of illness; the DRG classification system attempts to hold the latter constant. Horn et al. (1983) show that much of the variation within the DRGs can be explained with the use of a simple index of severity of the illness.

The system has also been criticized for providing hospitals with incentives to refuse to treat severely ill patients because hospitals that consistently treat the most severely ill patients within a DRG lose money on these patients. This may lead some hospitals, particularly proprietary hospitals, to refuse severely ill patients. Another major concern about the DRG payment system is that it may induce hospitals to discharge patients too early in order to keep costs below DRG payments, thereby reducing the quality of care.

At this point in time, it is difficult to obtain definitive results regarding the impact DRGs have had on hospitals, patients, and physicians. Initial findings suggest that DRGs have reduced the length of stay for Medicare patients, since the percentage decrease in the LOS is greater than those of earlier years. At the same time, the concern that DRGs may provide incentives to increase admissions does not seem to be empirically supported.

Disability-Related Categories

This section describes how Disability-Related Categories can be developed. Many of the issues raised can only be answered by an analysis of data on injured workers. The method that we suggest is a necessary first step toward such an analysis.

The DRGs are designed to identify similarities in work-loss days among workers with the same health problem. Although the DRCs' dependent variable is a duration of time similar to the DRGs, there are several different ways to characterize the time spent out of work. For example, consider the following sequence of time spent out of work for a hypothetical worker:

$$T_{ii} \qquad\qquad T_a \qquad T_d \qquad\qquad T_p \qquad T_e$$

_____x_____x_____x_____x_____x_____

                                                                     time

The worker is injured at time T_{ii}, is admitted to a hospital at time T_a, and discharged at time T_d. After a convalescent period, the worker is able to participate in the labor force at time T_p. Workers who cannot perform

Table 3-2.   Possible Dependent Variables

$LAW = T_e - T_{ii}$	Length of absence from work
$ALAW = LAW - LOS$	Adjusted length of absence from work equals length of absence from work minus length of stay
$LON = T_p - T_{ii}$	Length of nonparticipation
$ALON = LON - LOS$	Adjusted length of nonparticipation equals length of time out of work minus length of stay

their preinjury job or who have been replaced by a substitute worker will be unemployed for the period T_p to T_e. The dependent variable is best defined as the total length of absence from work (that is, $T_e - T_{ii} = LAW$), but other definitions can be used if a set of independent variables cannot be found to successfully reduce the variation in LAW. For example, the set of independent variables chosen may not adequately explain the duration of unemployment $(T_e - T_p)$. In this case, it would be better to eliminate the length of unemployment, $T_e - T_p = LOU$, from LAW to obtain the length of nonparticipation, $LON = LAW - LOU = T_p - T_{ii}$.

Another possibility is to eliminate the hospital stay from either LAW or LON on the premise that the DRG system can be used to decompose the length of hospital stays. This would result in an adjusted total time out of work, $ALAW = LAW - LOS$, and an adjusted length of nonparticipation, $ALON = LON - LOS$. If the DRC system uses ALAW or ALON as dependent variables, the DRG system would be used to assign lengths of stay in the hospital. Table 3-2 summarizes the four variables which might be used as dependent variables.

The independent variables will be more difficult to formulate without the benefit of some empirical analysis. Studies of the determinants of absence from work following an injury concentrate on the replacement ratio, the percentage of the wage that is replaced by the benefit, as one of the major determinants of absence from work (Fenn, 1981; Butler and Worrall, 1985). This variable cannot be used to define the DRCs since the DRCs will lead to a prospective payment of benefits.

On the basis of the literature that exists with respect to labor force participation and absence from work due to an illness or injury, the variables reported in table 3-3 have beem selected to be used as independent variables.

The classification into DRCs would probably be improved by using the Major Diagnostic Categories to initially partition the data set according to major body organ. At that point, a statistical technique such as regression

Table 3-3. Possible Independent Variables

Economic
Occupation
Wage rate/salary
Industry
Physical requirements of occupation
Health/Medical
Primary diagnosis
Secondary diagnosis
Severity of illness/injury
Hospital admission
Length of stay
Acute/chronic
Surgical procedure
Demographic
Age
Education

---

analysis could be used to further decompose the variation in absence from work. Figure 3-3 contains an hypothetical decomposition of all workers who have a fracture of a forearm. The physical requirements of the job, reflected in a categorization of occupations as manual or nonmanual, may prove to be the variable that initially reduces the variation in length of absence from work. For the group of workers in manual occupations, the characteristic of whether the fractured arm is the dominant arm further reduces the variation in LAW.

Applying the DRC System to Workers' Compensation

The DRC system, on its own, does not dictate how workers' compensation benefits such as a wage-loss benefit will be paid. The determination of benefits can be dealt with independently of the DRC system. This section discusses a method of establishing the length of time for which benefits would be paid and the likely impact of the DRC system on equity, adequacy and efficiency.

For a given DRC classification, the distribution in LAW will have a known mean, standard deviation, and percentiles such as the median. It is possible to use either the mean or a percentile as the basis for determining a prospective benefit. Since most of the distributions will be skewed

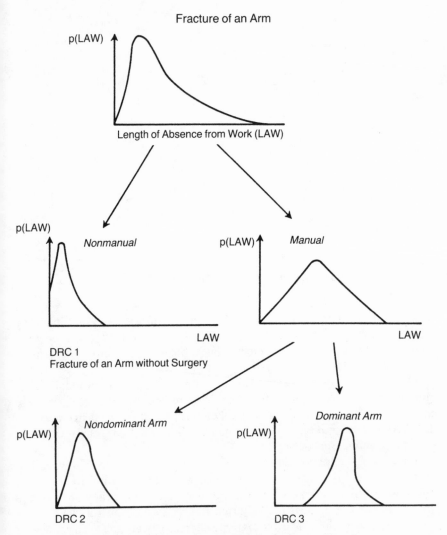

Figure 3-3. Decomposition of a Fracture of an Arm.

to the right, the mean will be greater than the median and will result in higher benefits.

For example, assume that the mean is used to establish benefits and further assume that a given DRC has a mean LAW of eight days. The benefit for a worker receiving a gross daily wage of $70.00 would be $560.00. This approach could be varied by incorporating the 66⅔ percent rule and minima and maxima benefits as is currently the case. An alternative to

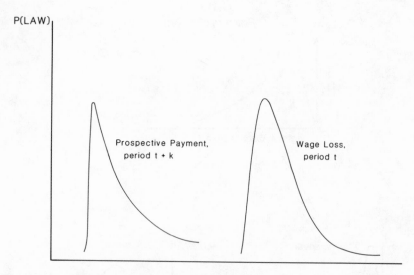

Figure 3-4.   Shift in Distribution of LAW Over Time.

the 66⅔ percent rule would be to use the net of tax wage multiplied by the mean LAW. These issues will be considered separately from the basic premise of the DRC system which is to establish a prospective payment on the basis of a classification system.

One of the major potential savings from DRCs is the gradual reduction in benefits over time as the classifications are updated. If the current system contains disincentive effects, then it is likely that the distributions in LAW will shift to the left after the benefits are switched from a wage-loss to a prospective approach.

Figure 3-4 compares the distribution in LAW based upon a wage-loss system with the distribution for the same workers under a DRC prospective benefit. Since workers differ in the degree to which they are affected by a wage-loss system, it is likely that the mean and the standard deviation of the wage-loss distribution will decrease over time. This suggests that as the DRC standard deviations decrease, the benefits will become more equitable.

By eliminating fee-for-service reimbursement, the DRG approach eliminates incentives to provide more services than are necessary for the welfare of the patient. The adequacy of health care is maintained by the requirement that health care producers meet standards defined by the funding agencies. DRCs may reduce workers' compensation expenditures by eliminating work disincentives and reducing the costs of administering claims.

Because DRCs change the amount and distribution of benefits, the savings must be compared to the changes which DRC creates in the adequacy of benefits or in the equity with which they are distributed.

An important feature of the DRC system will be the degree to which the benefits are equitable. The DRG system can work equitably for hospitals if the average payment to the hospital equals the average cost. The fact that a hospital may be seriously undercompensated in some cases is not a major problem as long as cases exist which sufficiently overcompensate the hospital. Obviously, the same claim cannot be made for DRCs. It can be expected that the vast majority of workers will submit one claim, so an equity-through-averaging approach is not feasible.

A method exists, however, to improve the equity of the DRC System. Hospitals are provided additional compensation if a patient stays in the hospital more than 1.94 standard deviations above the mean, or generates costs in excess of 50 percent above the mean, for their DRG. The equity and adequacy of the system will improve if workers can obtain extended benefits for outlier durations of absence from work. Qualifying as an outlier can also be targeted to a specified number of standard deviations above the mean. By the same token, a reduction in benefits should be considered for workers who may be considered inliers, where the actual duration is far below the mean for the DRC.

Conclusions

We described how the DRG method could be modified to apply to workplace injury and illness rather than to medical care. The DRC method promises to reduce expenditures for temporary disability claims and provide a more equitable distribution of payments for permanent partial disabilities. The method cannot be applied to permanent total disability claims because the number of claims is too small.

There are some important questions about DRCs that we have not discussed. One question is whether temporary disability benefits should be calculated by combining current benefits to DRC durations or whether the benefit formulae should be different in a DRC system. The choice depends upon the reasons for the 66⅔ percent rule and eligibility criteria such as the waiting period. If these rules are designed to offset moral hazard by forcing workers to coinsure against wage losses, they could be eliminated in a successful DRC system. Benefits could be paid for full wage loss but limited to the number of days indicated by the relevant DRC. If the purpose of the 66⅔ percent rule is to adjust gross wages for income taxes, it need not change if DRCs are adopted. It seems likely that the rule serves both objectives.

We suggest that DRC benefits be calculated on the basis of gross wages adjusted for income taxes using the average rates on gross income in the state in which the worker lives. Although workers with above-average deductions suffer from such a rule, it promises substantial increases in administrative efficiency. The net social benefit can only be calculated by simulating the effects of DRCs on actual populations of injured workers.

Many states legislate maxima and minima for WC benefits. These limits address the distribution of income rather than work incentives. Implementing DRCs would not require changes in the benefit limits.

DRCs could be adjusted, over time, to incorporate the observed effects of existing DRCs on duration of work absences within each DRC and the adequacy and equity of compensation payments among injured workers. The DRCs could, in other words, be experience-rated, providing insurers, labor, and management with a factual basis for discussing changes in workers' compensation laws. If the interested parties could agree on standards for adequacy and equity, experience rating of DRCs could be used to adjust workers' compensation benefits without requiring amendments to workers' compensation laws.

A successful DRC approach to wage-loss benefits could produce the information needed to set more accurate coinsurance limits, creating a simpler and hopefully less litigious WC system. The evolution of the WC system could proceed without the long lags inherent in the current process of legislative review and amendment. The process would also supply substantially more information than is now available to state legislatures when they revise WC statutes.

Although imperfect, our proposal must be evaluated against current practices rather than an ideal. Workers' compensation benefits are set without the benefit of any objective data on work incentives and with limited information on the adequacy and equity of compensation. At worst, the DRC system would require the states to systematically collect and analyze data on the relationship between benefit-programs and the work days lost by injured workers.[6] We suggest that states considering wage-loss benefit schemes carefully consider the possible advantages of the DRC method.

Our discussion is speculative. If the DRC concept is attractive to WC plans, an intelligent decision on the merits of DRCs requires good estimates of their benefits and costs. The problems with scheduled benefits are an important reminder of the difficulty of converting the complex relationship between impairments, wages, and work to a manageable set of administrative rules. The impact of DRCs on the adequacy and equity of benefits should be simulated, using data on current PPD benefits before the method is implemented. The costs of errors can be minimized by restricting, for some time, the application of DRCs to temporary disability claims where wage losses and program expenditures are relatively small.

The discussion also shows that DRCs could be an important component of the wage-loss systems that are being discussed as replacements for scheduled benefits. Before states adopt wage-loss plans, they should consider the opportunity to establish DRCs by collecting data on current recipients of scheduled benefits. The opportunity can be lost if the shift to wage-loss benefits is made on the basis of hope rather than on a good understanding of how the current system works and how DRCs might improve it.

The opportunity to create DRCs is likely to disappear over time. Since most states still rely on scheduled benefits, it is possible to collect data on duration of absence from work and use it to create DRCs for different impairments and different severities of impairment.

The chance to obtain data on absence from work among the recipients of scheduled benefits should not be ignored. DRCs based on data in which work disincentives are minimal offer the possibility of efficient but equitable benefits for all types of permanent partial impairments. If states continue to adopt wage-loss benefits, the chance to create these DRCs will disappear. We suggest that the opportunity should not be lost.

Notes

1 That is, a one-percent increase in the ratio of benefits to wages (evaluated at the means) reduces the number of lost days by .09 percent.

2 The recent study by the California Workers' Compensation Institute (see CWCI Bulletin, April 1, 1985) supports this view. It shows that "regardless of age, workers with the least disability are compensated best."

3 The results are also conditioned on the specific characteristic of the New York schedule. Since New York is one of the few states that also pays wage-loss benefits ("nonscheduled benefits") for certain partial disabilities, the results cannot be easily generalized to other states.

4 Johnson and Curington, 1986.

5 The estimates assume that wage losses end at age 65 and that wage loss equals the product of preinjury earnings and duration of absence from work. Wage losses are not reduced for Social Security Disability benefits, and the disincentive effects of wage-loss benefits are not considered.

6 Many states collect most of the data needed to operate a DRC system.

References

Berkowitz, Monroe and John Burton. "The Transformation of Flordia to a Wage Loss State." Chapter 10 in *Permanent Disability Benefits in the Workers' Com-*

pensation Program: A Multistate Study of Criteria and Procedures. Mimeo (Draft to November 1983).

Berkowitz, Monroe, and William G. Johnson. "Health and Labor Force Participation." *Journal of Human Resources,* Winter 1974: 117–128.

Burton, John F., Jr., and Wayne Vroman. "A Report on Permanent Partial Disabilities Under Workers' Compensation." *Research Report of the Interdepartmental Workers' Compensation Task Force* 6, Washington, D.C.: U.S. Department of Labor Employment Standards Administration (1979): 11–77.

Butler, Richard J., and J.D. Worrall. "Work Injury Compensation and the Duration of Nonwork Spells," *The Economic Journal,* September 1985: 714–724.

Butler, Richard J., and J.D. Worrall. *Workers' Compensation Benefit and Injury Claims Rates in the Seventies.* National Council on Compensation Insurance, October 1981, Mimeo.

California Workers' Compensation Institute. *Bulletin,* April 1, 1985.

Chelius, James R. "The Influence of Workers' Compensation on Safety Incentive." *Industrial and Labor Relations Review* 35, 2 (January 1982): 235–242.

Chirikos, Thomas N., and Gilbert Nestel. "Economic Determinants and Consequences of Self-Reported Work Disability." *Journal of Health Economics* 3 (1984): 117–136.

Fenn, Paul. "Sickness Duration, Residual Disability, and Income Replacement: An Empirical Analysis," *Economic Journal,* March 1981: 158–173.

Fetter, Robert B., Youngsoo Shin, Jean L. Freeman, Richard F. Averill, and John A. Thompson. "Case Mix Definition by Diagnosis-Related Groups," *Medical Care,* February 1980.

Horn, Susan D., and Phoebe D. Sharkey. "Measuring Severity of Illness to Predict Patient Resource Use within DRGs." *Inquiry,* Winter 1983.

Jarvis, Kenneth A. *A Model for Measuring the Adequacy of Washington State's Workmen's Compensation Cash Benefits in Cases of Temporary Total Disability.* Unpublished DBA Dissertation, University of Washington, 1971.

Johnson, William G., and William P. Curington. "Wage Losses and Workers' Compensation Benefits 1970–1980." In Research Papers of the *New York State Temporary Commission on Workers' Compensation and Disability Benefits,* Albany, NY, April 1986.

Johnson, William G. "Perspectives on Wage Loss Benefits for Workers' Compensation Pensioners in Ontario." Metropolitan Studies Program, Labor and Health Series Occasional Paper No. 1, The Maxwell School. Syracuse, NY: Syracuse University, September 1986.

Johnson, William G. "The Disincentive Effects of Worker's Compensation Insurance." In John D. Worrall (ed.), *Safety and the Work Force: Incentives and Disincentives in Worker's Compensation Insurance.* Ithaca, NY: ILR Press, 1983.

Jolivette, David. "Temporary Benefits under Workmen's Compensation: A Need for Change." *Wisconsin Law Review* 69, 3 (1969): 949–968.

Larson, Arthur. "The Wage Loss Principle in Workers' Compensation." *William Mitchell Law Review* 6 (1980): 501–532.

Mills, Ronald, Robert B. Fetter, Donald C. Riedel, and Richard Averill. "AUTO-

GRP: An Interactive Computer System for the Analysis of Health Care Data." *Medical Care*, July 1976.

NYS Workers' Compensation Board. *Compensated Cases Closed, 1982*. Research and Statistics Bulletin No. 43, New York State Workers' Compensation Board.

Parsons, Donald O. "Health, Family Structure, and Labor Supply." *American Economic Review*, September 1977: 703–712.

Prospective Payment Assessment Commission. *Report and Recommendations to the Secretary*. U.S. Department of Health and Human Services, Washington, DC: U.S. Government Printing Office, April 1, 1985.

Prospective Payment Assessment Commission. *Technical Appendixes to the Report and Recommendations to the Secretary*. U.S. Department of Health and Human Services, Washington, DC: U.S. Government Printing Office, April 1, 1985.

Sherman, P. Tecumseh. "The Basis of Compensation." In the U.S. Department of Labor, *Proceedings of the Conference on Social Insurance*. IAIABC, Washington, DC, U.S.G.P.O., December 1916: 184–193.

Weiler, Paul C. *Protecting the Worker from Disability: Challenges for the Eighties*. Ontario Government Press, April 1983.

Yelin, Edward, Michael Nevitt, and Wallace Epstein. "Toward an Epidemiology of Work Disability." *Milbank Memorial Fund Quarterly*, Summer 1980: 386–415.

4 COMPENSATING VICTIMS OF OCCUPATIONAL DISEASES: CAN WE STRUCTURE AN EFFECTIVE POLICY?

Harris Schlesinger
Emilio C. Venezian

Workers afflicted with occupational injury or disease are compensated for their losses in a variety of ways. The mechanism that is most often considered is workers' compensation insurance which, under suitable conditions, provides compensation for such losses without regard to fault on the part of the employer. Workers may also be compensated through the existence of wage differentials related to the anticipated losses or to the portion of those losses not properly compensated from other sources. In addition, victims of occupational injury or disease may obtain compensation through the tort system if the cause of injury or disease is a product whose producer has failed to provide it in a safe form or with suitable warnings regarding the dangers involved in its use. Other sources of compensation include private disability insurance, private health and accident insurance, and payments under public programs such as Social Security. This paper discusses the problems associated with structuring a reasonable system of compensation for occupational disease in a context in which various sources of compensation exist.[1]

Compensating the victims of occupational diseases poses several problems in addition to those ordinarily associated with compensating the victims of other workplace accidents. Quite often, the number of diseased workers affected is large, the source of exposure to the disease is not clear, and the manifestation and/or discovery of the disease is delayed over time. These factors add complexities to the already complex issues surrounding questions of financial responsibility. The recent publicity given to asbestos-related diseases and the bankruptcy filing of Manville Corporation have served to heighten public awareness of some of these problems. Any system of compensation for victims of these diseases must look toward the joint goals of fair and efficient compensation on the one hand, and providing the incentives necessary to maintain a safe work environment on the other. This paper strives toward establishing such a system.

Any set of rules regarding the responsibility for untoward events will affect the way in which agents choose to act in pursuit of their self-interest. If the rules impose all the costs of untoward events on the users of a product, the manufacturer will have only secondary reasons for making a safe product whereas the user will have strong incentives to select safe products and use them sparingly. At the other extreme, if the manufacturer is deemed responsible for all untoward effects, the user will have no incentive to select safe products or to use them safely whereas the manufacturer will have direct incentives to produce safe products. The existence of financing mechanisms such as insurance and even the way in which such financing mechanisms are priced also have effects on who bears the cost of unsafe products and, ultimately, on what level of safety will be selected.

The selection of safety levels in the workplace is also influenced by the rules that are developed to allocate financial responsibility. If workers were to be required to bear all the consequences of untoward events, we might expect to find that workers select their opportunities for employment with great care and exact higher wages from employers that have records of high frequencies of severe accidents. Employers, for their part, would be acting rationally if they devoted to safety only as much as is required to offset the effect of lower labor supply. If, on the other hand, employers are responsible for all the financial burden of untoward events, they would allocate to safety as much as is required to just offset the declining cost of accidents; workers should then be indifferent among employers that use the same methods of production.

In this paper we attempt to provide a framework for evaluating the effect of rules on the allocation of financial responsibility on safety levels in the workplace, paying particular attention to the problems associated with occupational disease.

Some Limitations of Previous Studies

Many studies have been published on the effects of rules for the allocation of financial responsibility on the way in which safety levels are chosen.[2]

For the most part, these studies have related either to issues of product safety, which is covered under the tort system, or of workplace injuries resulting from sudden and clearly identifiable events in the workplace, which are usually covered by workers' compensation under a system which is basically no-fault.

Many issues related to occupational disease, however, are quite different from those related to occupational injuries. Two major factors account for this difference: (1) long-term exposure is often involved in the development of the disease, and (2) exposures leading to the disease might be encountered both in the workplace and elsewhere. Moreover, these two factors may interact.

As an example, consider the relationship between noise and hearing impairment.[3] The extent of damage to hearing increases as the level of sound increases and as the duration of the exposure increases. Intermittent exposure is less damaging than constant exposure, and periods of relative silence tend to reduce or limit the amount of damage. Instances of impaired hearing from exposure to noise will not occur immediately after exposure. Typically it may taken 10 or 20 years for impairment to be functionally significant. This lapse of time by itself distinguishes this example from the types of injuries discussed in the literature. In addition, there is the problem that the worker may expose herself to high sound levels by frequenting disco bars or engaging in motorcycle races. Thus the relative effects of the workplace exposure and the voluntary exposure become an issue. Finally, there is an interaction, in that high sound levels on the job will cause temporary hearing loss and contribute to the need for playing music or conducting conversations at a level of sound higher than would otherwise be used. The paradigms used in the literature adapt poorly to such circumstances. Other occupational disease exposures, such as asbestos, cotton dust, coal dust, and stress, differ in detail from the example presented above, but retain many of the features that distinguish it from the models of occupational injury.

Effects that occur long after exposure have been discussed in a number of papers, both in the context of product liability and workplace safety. Most of the discussion has centered on events that have a brief duration, such as a sudden release of radioactivity or a carcinogenic substance. Though the consequences of these events may not become apparent for a long time, the timing of the event and the parties at play are both clearly identifiable. When the exposure itself is protracted, however, it is not nearly as easy to identify the parties at issue, especially if the business line which causes the exposure is one in which the turnover of labor is high. A well-known example comes from the mining of radioactive ores in the postwar period in the United States. The average tenure of a miner in a given uranium mine is said to have been about four years whereas the average lag from exposure to radioactivity to overt cancer is around 25 years. Thus, determining the relative responsibility of the various employers is no trivial matter. Similar problems are common in exposure to asbestos. Many of these problems are discussed by Danzon (1984), Epstein (1984), and Viscusi (1984).

These problems stem from a variety of sources. A key one is the fact that when exposure is cumulative the effects are not necessarily additive. If we expose a worker to asbestos this year and you expose the same worker to asbestos next year, the health consequences will not be the same as they would be if the exposures had been to two different workers. The issue of responsibility is greatly complicated by nonadditivity. Basically we should recognize that, under these conditions, we are dealing with externalities and that these effects cannot be addressed from a perspective of property rights, which covers only private goods. The externalities we are dealing with are, in essence, public harms. It is not our intent in this paper to create a new system of allocation based on the economics of public goods; areas in which nonadditivity is important will, however, be duly noted. As a rule, nonadditivity creates a need for identifying the prior exposures of individual workers and using that information in subsequent decisions. Though there may be strong economic incentives to promote rational decision making (given the information), there may also be rational objectives that create barriers to the flow of information. An individual who is at high risk of developing lung cancer or emphysema because of personal habits (such as smoking) or individual characteristics (such as genetic antitrypsin deficiency) and has been exposed to asbestos in one setting may well object to being barred from working in other environments that create a health hazard that is very small in the specific instance but that provides the expectation of substantial compensation if the disease were to become manifest.

Another limitation of the existing literature on the subject of safety incentives is the artificial separation of tort systems and no-fault systems. While under some conditions it may be worthwhile to assume that the employer is only an employer, in the case of some of the gradual exposures that result in injury related to employment there is also the possibility that injury will result from the employer's role as a producer. The courts already recognize this "dual capacity" theory as one way around the workers' compensation laws. Asbestos is a typical example of the coupling between the employer in the role of employer and the employer as a producer. A company such as Manville Corporation would have derived no benefit from exposing workers to asbestos dust in the course of manufacturing asbestos products if it were not for the fact that asbestos products were used by others. If the use of the product results in potential exposure of users, the company may bear financial responsibility for untoward health effects in both the workplace and the marketplace. The financial responsibility for these two types of effect is, under current practice, subject to different rules. It would be unrealistic to asume that the company performs separate analyses for setting safety policy in these two segments and ignores the interactions. It is more reasonable to assume that the company will recognize that some policies may make sense from one perspective but not from the other. Thus, if information comes to light on the potential harm of a particular kind of exposure, the company might have every incentive to disclose the fact and take remedial action to minimize the effect on current employees and future users, but might find itself bankrupt if the tort rules impose on it the financial responsibility under product liability for all past users of the product. Ignoring the possibility of such interactions may result in grossly misleading conclusions.

Another area that is affected by the assumed relation between exposure and effect is the ability to collect information and draw conclusions. In the case of sudden toxic releases of short duration, it is conceivable to keep track of the exposed population and measure the health effects, although there may be a big gap between conceiving such an activity and carrying it out (as demonstrated by the recent Union Carbide mishap in Bhopal). In the case of gradual exposure, this activity can hardly be entertained seriously unless we anticipate ex ante that there will be a gradual exposure, that the exposure will be harmful, and that we know all alternate sources of simultaneous exposures. A meaningful analysis of the data would also require detailed knowledge of the alternate sources of exposure among the population under study and of models that relate the timing and severity of exposure to the resultant health effects. As an example of the problems that are likely to be encountered, consider that most of the studies of the health effects of caffeine are based on information on consumption of coffee and tea and ignore two major sources of caffeine consumption in the U.S.: cola beverages and analgesics. Thus, the existence of any reliable information is likely to be a problem. It is, therefore, a mistake to assume that all effects are known accurately in trying to assess the relative value of various rules in providing incentives to behave in ways that we may view as socially acceptable.

Finally, it is a mistake to assume, as much of the existing literature has done, that we can define unambiguously what constitutes socially optimal behavior. The structure of the problem is so complex that the existence of a best solution should be proven rather than assumed, and if there is no best solution, as turns out to be the case, alternate methods for evaluating rules must be adopted.

Issues in Financing Reparations

Recently, 34 asbestos producers and 16 insurance companies signed the so-called Wellington Agreement. This agreement, named after its principal designer, Yale Law School Dean Harry Wellington, establishes a mechanism for handling asbestos-related damage claims. Only one month after this signing, Manville Corporation, the most well-known litigant in the asbestos arena and a company which was not a signer of the Wellington Agreement, announced its establishment of a similar method for handling asbestos-related claims. Both of these events underscore the unsatisfactory workings of extant mechanisms in dealing with asbestos-related damages. This dissatisfaction stems from two sources. One is the enormous financial burden that can build up rapidly and unexpectedly in tort cases involving occupational disease. For example, prior to the setting up of these claims mechanisms, the estimated value of claims against asbestos manufacturers had exceeded the sum of their financial resources plus the financial resources of their insurers by more than one billion dollars.[4] The second source of dissatisfaction is the high transaction cost involved in settling these claims. Of the one billion dollars spent on asbestos-related claims from the early 1970s to the end of 1982, some $560 million had gone to defending the cases, $40 million to litigation among organizations regarding insurance coverage and liability, $164 million to pay for plaintiffs' legal fees, and only $236 million to pay net compensation to the plaintiffs.[5]

Potential Bankruptcy

If existing claims exhaust the ability of the system, either through limits of insurer liability or through protection of manufacturers by bankruptcy laws, there will be no recourse available for possible later claimants. Exhaustion of the system may create inequities that favor those who can settle claims early, while excluding equally deserving claims that arise too late to make a claim against the assets of the producers and insurers. The problem of insolvency appears minor in the case of workers' compensation because most states require the interposition of third-party insurers and make provision for state guarantee funds. The validity of such guarantees, however, is largely predicated on the notion that the present methods of dealing with occupational disease will continue to be acceptable. If current limitations on coverage were lifted by a court decision and the corresponding liabilities were of the order of magnitude of those encountered in asbestos-related cases, real doubt might arise regarding the ability and willingness of state funds to cover the resulting financial obligations.

The most famous particular example is that of Manville Corporation (formerly Johns–Manville), which surprised the financial and legal communities on August 26, 1982 with its Chapter 11 filing. It was the first time that a financially healthy company had turned to the U.S. Bankruptcy Code to protect itself from future economic ruin. Several other asbestos manufacturers have also recently filed under Chapter 11. Manville was profitable at the time of its filing and has gotten even more profitable since. In the first half of 1985, Manville's net earnings were $32.6 million on revenues of $993.9 million. However, the company also faces some $112 *billion* in liability claims including some 20,000 claims for asbestos-related diseases worth more than $29 billion—although some people contend that Manville may have exaggerated its future liabilities to help its Chapter 11 cause.

While the above statistics for Manville Corporation give some idea of the financial impact involved, we note that Manville is only one of many defendants involved in asbestos-related disease claims. We also note that there exist many other causes of occupational disease in addition to the cause of exposure to asbestos. Some of these causes have received a great deal of attention in attempting solutions, such as black lung disease, which precipitated the Black Lung Benefits Act of 1969. This Act has been amended frequently since that time. Other causes, such as exposure to Agent Orange, which has received much recent publicity, have not had special systems fully established for compensating victims. And indeed many other occupational diseases abound. The Bureau of Labor Statistics documents approximately 162,000 occupational illnesses each year, a figure which likely understates the true number.[6]

Finally, we point out that although this chapter is directed primarily towards occupational safety, it also has general implications for the use of hazardous products in the workplace in general. Workers frequently file suits against the producers of such hazardous products as a means of circumventing the limited recompensing of workers' compensation insurance. This is possible even when the manufacturer of the hazardous product and the employer are one and the same through the so-called dual capacity theory.[7]

Transaction Costs

Manville Corporation had already paid close to $50 million in legal fees and court costs from the time its Chapter 11 proceedings began through the beginning of 1986. However, these costs were paid in part to set up its present system, and a chief goal of its present system is to reduce costs of future litigation. This is understandable when one considers the high transaction costs of compensating victims through the current system. In products liability insurance, for example, only about 37.5 cents out of every premium dollar goes to compensate victims. The remainder goes to insurer operating costs and to legal costs.[8] Furthermore, even these costs would underestimate the costs associated with paying out claims dollars, since they do not include costs such as lost wages and transportation costs for court appearances.

Another cost is the cost of unfiled claims. If the compensation system is somewhat complex, many individuals might feel intimidated by it. Perhaps they would experience some disutility in seeking recompense for an occupational injury. For example, someone might prefer not to testify in court; or they might not appreciate having their background history researched; or they may wish to simply forget about some untoward event rather than be forced to recall the details of their mishap over and over again. While such costs do not show up on a company's balance sheet, they are nonetheless costs imposed on society by the frictions within the compensation-seeking mechanisms; and as such these costs could perhaps be viewed as a type of social transaction costs.

The Nature of Exposures

Multiple Causes and Sources

If our compensation mechanism for occupational diseases and injuries is based in part on the contribution of workplace conditions to the resulting disease or injury, a problem arises as to what that contribution might be. Much attention has focused on the problem of determining who ought to pay for occupational disease cases. One of the major problems is determining the source of exposure. If we were dealing with a well-defined accident with immediately recognizable untoward consequences, we could focus on the questions of negligence (if a negligence tort standard is extant), work relatedness (if a workers' compensation hearing is invovled) and/or the degree of compensation. However, the cause of many occupational diseases is harder to determine since no accident per se may have occurred. Instead the exposure might have taken place over a period of time and might have been from one of a number of different possible sources. As such, it underscores the distinction between the terms *accident* and *occurrence* in the language of insurance policies.[9]

The usual problems involved with showing negligence apply if we seek recourse under a negligence torts standard. Even with a strict liability theory of torts, many problems are encountered in occupational disease cases. For example, there might be numerous potential causes of a disease, and indeed it is highly likely that several of these potential causes were jointly responsible for the disease. It may be impossible, however, to determine which of the potential causes was actually responsible or to what degree each cause is actually responsible. In this regard, we might be faced with an irreducible uncertainty.

To complicate matters, we might have not only multiple causes of the onset of the disease, but also multiple sources for each cause, multiple employers as potential contributors to the onset of the disease, and perhaps the lifestyle of the individual as another contributing factor. For example, smoking cigarettes is known to increase the risk of asbestos-related diseases.[10] Some diseases, such as cancer and coronary disease, could obviously come from a number of possible on- and off-the-job exposures. The possibility also exists that the disease was caused by exposure to several different substances and/or conditions, any one of which would have been harmless in isolation.[11] How should we apportion financial responsibility in a situation such as this?

The complexity of the problem is compounded by the observation that multiple causes often do not provide additive contributions. In many instances the risk from exposure to multiple causes is close to multiplicative. Smoking, for example, increases the risk of lung cancer by a factor of ten in people who are not exposed to asbestos and by the same factor in people exposed to a given level of asbestos.[12] Asbestos itself increases the risk of lung cancer by the same factor in people of various ages. This characteristic implies that the marginal contribution of a given exposure depends on all other exposures and cannot be easily isolated.

Given these elements, the way in which financial responsibility should be apportioned is not clear. The apportionment rules will have an important bearing on the deterrent value of the system and on the resulting allocation of resources.

Time Delays

The problems associated with determining the cause of a disease are exacerbated, in the case of occupational diseases, by long latency periods and the intertemporal nature of the exposures. Also, new problems are created by these time lapses. For example, consider a disease that is not manifested, or at least not diagnosed, until 20 years after exposure at a former workplace. The employer responsible for the exposure may have been out of existence for quite some time. Its records might no longer be available to establish the liability of insurers. If financial responsibility is questionable, the passage of time will cause the case to suffer from deteriorating evidence and increasing complexity because of subsequent additional exposures. Furthermore, a statute of limitations that has run out may not allow a suit to be filed.[13]

Determining financial responsibility is complicated still further when the worker has been exposed to hazards at several different work sites, a situation that becomes more and more likely with the passage of time. The problem compounds itself, since even if we were somehow able to pick out a single place of employment where the exposure took place, this exposure might have occurred over the course of several years. As such, there might have been several changes in corporate structure and many insurers may have provided liability coverage to the employer. The problem also exists as to how we should apportion financial responsibility among the several insurers. This allocation of financial responsibility is complicated by the intricate layering of primary and excess insurers and by the exhaustion of policy limits in specific years in jurisdictions that hold liability to be joint and several. Much of the current turmoil in asbestos-related disease, for example, involves interpreting the language in insurance contracts written many years earlier.

Effective Deterrence

Incentives for Optimal Safety

Any system of compensation for occupational diseases affects employer behavior. Much of the literature in law and economics that addresses the question of liability for occupational diseases emphasizes the incentives the system provides for achieving an efficient level of safety in the workplace.[14] Ideally, the compensation system should provide incentives for employers to provide a safe work environment.

Penalizing firms on the basis of current standards provides a dubious incentive if the employer's actions were consistent with standards and norms at the time the exposure occurred. Epstein (1984) addresses this point, noting that, "(I)t is highly unwise to allow suits with the properties so common in modern tort litigation, in which a jury determines the standards for safe products while simultaneously determining whether a given product meets the standards just set."[15] The obvious problem here is that the standards are set around the circumstances involved in the claim which is being decided, so that an ex ante decision by the employer to comply (or not to comply) with this set of standards is impossible. A problem which may be even more serious is that this system of penalties provides a deterrent to the improvement of standards by employers who may face a large liability if they establish the likelihood that some practice or exposure creates a hazard in the workplace.

A related issue deals with the fact that technology is constantly changing, so that standards that existed at the time exposure to some occupational disease occurred will, most likely, be different from the standards of today. Our concern should be primarily with providing incentives to meet current standards and to improve those standards rather than focusing on what could have been done with knowledge that has developed since the exposure took place. Of course, the penalties for past violations signal employers as to how strict the system is in enforcing its standards. These signals help to deter unsatisfactory performance by employers subject to today's standards.[16]

Incentives for Claims Filing

There is another side to the incentive issue, namely the incentives provided for the worker to file false or exaggerated claims. In some ways, the tort system and systems of insurance encourage these claims. Contingent fees, easy access to the courts and the near non-existence of countercharges for frivolous suits make it easy for claimants to seek excessive damage awards. Of course, the so-called "deep pockets" theory of jury decision making cannot be disregarded here, where jury awards are often partially based on ability to compensate. The current system provides an incentive to file late in the course of the disease (subject to statute of limitation constraints) since this strategy maximizes both the award size if the case is won and the probability of winning. This incentive might be particularly problematic for diseases viewed as incurable. This late filing could delay the development of cures, rehabilitation, and methods of limiting the further development of the disease.

We also have the usual types of moral hazard issues that arise in cases of asymmetric information. A fully covered worker might not take the proper on-the-job precautions, knowing that losses will be compensated. In addition, there is a moral hazard involved in determining the facts leading to the onset of the disease. For example, would the workman who had just been inadvertently exposed to a mild dose of radiation on the job find it in his interest to mention to his employer that he had been with his girl-friend, who is a nurse, the night before at a secret rendezvous at the hospital and that they secretly met in the X-ray room with the equipment accidently turned on?

Of course, there might exist disincentives for filing claims (especially claims that are not too large) if the procedures involved are expensive, time-consuming, tedious or embarrassing. A workman rendered impotent by a work-related exposure might be reluctant to seek recourse if it involves explaining to a jury or review panel (perhaps over and over again) the details of his impairment as well as defending the countercharge that he is only experiencing personal, psychological, sexual problems, and facing the possibility that disclosure of the condition might affect the quality of his life.

The Role of Information and Insurance

The asymmetry of information creates several problems. On the one hand, we have the moral hazard problem, where the workers have incentives to file claims that would not be justified based on full information. But the employer also is in a position to know and withhold information. The employee probably knows only as much information as available statistics show and the employer is willing to disclose as public information. If an employer can reduce future claims by being "unaware" of certain work-place hazards, it can choose to ignore information concerning these hazards so that it can later claim it was unaware of them.

The fact that both the employer and the employee may have insurance complicates matters. The employer's insurance may provide incentives for moral hazard by the employer. For example, regulations or legal precedents which raise standards of due care and make it easier to prove employers did not exercise due care can have the effect of actually lowering the level of care used and causing a substitution of increased insurance purchases—hardly the intended effect.[17]

Additionally, the nature of the exposure to hazards which caused the disease for a particular individual is often uncertain. Questions arise as to which parties should be held financially responsible. The employer's behavior ex post of the discovery of a disease might, at least in part, be directed towards establishing insurer liability. At the same time, insurers will make an effort to show that they are not liable. Thus, some resources are directed towards establishing this potential liability of insurers—resources which could be used more productively elsewhere.

Appropriate Compensation

Disparity Among Compensations

Unless compensation is decided on a case-by-case basis by an entity with complete information and ultimate wisdom, we are bound to have some individuals with similar claims compensated differently. Asymmetric information precludes complete knowledge so we cannot expect to compensate all individuals optimally (assuming we know what is "optimal" compensation). Although this situation might be minimized if the system induces all parties involved to reveal truthfully their private information, it cannot be guaranteed that providing such incentives is consistent with basic efficiency conditions.[18] As a result, one individual might receive a million-dollar award while a similarly situated co-worker, whose case is heard by a different jury or review panel, might have the case dismissed due to insufficient evidence.

The existence of potential disparity may encourage behavior that is aimed at affecting the compensation system itself rather than towards more productive uses. For example, a diseased worker may prefer to forego the optimal level of therapy prior to a hearing in order to gain sympathy for his or her current state of being. The asymmetry of information and the adversarial system of review (especially if it is the courts) provide incentives to all parties to overstate their respective cases.

Taken to the extreme, the system can suffer in general from two basic types of errors: (1) compensating undeserving victims (undeserving from a standpoint of causation) and (2) not compensating deserving victims. Obviously both types of errors are bound to occur. Moreover, the above description over simplifies the situation, which in reality is continuous. Thus, we should talk about over- and under-compensating various victims, under- and overcharging various potentially responsible parties, and the degree to which they are incorrectly compensated or incorrectly assessed for injury.

Even if we reduce some of the discrepancies by going to scheduled awards, as suggested by Danzon (1984), we retain the asymmetry of information and cannot guarantee that using the schedule will eliminate disparity, especially since schedules are finite whereas the set of possible outcomes forms a continuum. It may also be true that outcomes very near to each other in this continuum are placed quite far apart on our discrete compensation schedules.[19]

We also have discrepancies which are created by time and space. For example, workers' compensation lump-sum benefits for certain mishaps exhibit large differences among the various jurisdictions. In 1981, the loss of an arm at the shoulder brought a lump-sum award of $10,100 in North Dakota, whereas the same injury brought an award of $142,347 in the District of Columbia and an award of $225,507 to someone who was a federal employee. Workers' compensation benefits for other scheduled injuries and permanent total disability show similar differences among jurisdictions. The point is that even the use of scheduled awards does not eliminate the variance inherent in the system.

No Compensation and Multiple Compensation

Even if the level of compensation could be determined with perfect information, a financial-responsibility system might be limited by bankruptcy considerations. Landes and Posner (1984), for example, show how bankruptcy constraints alter the incentives of employers to provide a safe workplace. Viscusi (1984) points out how a bankrupt firm also leaves its former workers who later develop disease conditions with no former employer left to sue. More generally, the effectiveness of any mechanism that depends upon ex post compensation from a previous employer needs to consider the employer's ability to pay when required. One needs to realize that such an employer may no longer exist, either because of an earlier bankruptcy or due to a myriad of other possible reasons, or if it does exist might not own sufficient resources to pay all claims.[20]

If a former employer is the only source of compensation, we have just discussed how it is possible that no compensation might be forthcoming. However, there are quite often multiple sources of compensation. Some of these may be via public welfare programs, some via insurance policies, some via torts awards, and still others via implicit contracts such as premiums for risk that might be built into the wage structure.

Public welfare programs usually provide assistance to the diseased individual without regard to the cause.[21] For example, public medical assistance and/or assistance from private foundations directed towards particular diseases might provide medical and therapeutic care and advice for no or nominal charges. Social Security Disability Insurance (SSDI), Medicare, and Medicaid, for example, do not concern themselves with fault in allocating benefits. In addition to this public assistance, many employers provide private medical and/or disability insurance coverages to their employees. Furthermore, employees may opt to purchase additional insurance coverage on a private basis. Some workers might also have disability provisions within their private pension plans. Additionally, some workers may have coverage through accidental death and dismemberment insurance (ADD), which provides lump-sum scheduled benefits, or through dismemberment provisions in their life insurance policies.

These benefits, along with those that are (at least in theory) related to the cause of the disease, such as workers' compensation insurance and tort awards, interact with each other in various ways. For example, successful tort actions enable the employer to recover (through various legal mechanisms) any workers' compensation payments. However, SSDI benefits are not recoverable in this way; and ADD benefits are paid regardless of other compensation. Thus, it is possible for injured workers to receive nonoffsetting awards from different sources. The total of all awards might leave the individual financially better off following the disease than had the disease not occurred. This possible overcompensation will be exacerbated if the predisease wage level already included a premium for bearing job-related risks. Thus, the worker might end up being compensated both ex ante (through this risk premium) as well as ex post.[22]

Issues in the Design of Efficient Compensation

Basic Considerations of Efficiency

In theory, we desire a compensation system for occupational disease that equates the marginal benefits and marginal costs of the induced level of safety in the workplace. The usual problems associated with measuring costs and benefits apply in the area of occupational disease—perhaps to an even greater extent than usual. We are also confronted with problems associated with asymmetric information as discussed previously. Even if we could somehow circumvent these informational and measurement problems, we are still at an impasse in defining a collective set of value judgments for society, as is clear from the well-known results of Arrow (1951).

Given the above types of limitations, a more workable criterion is that developed by Danzon. She defines efficiency as the "minimization of costs from four sources: injuries, injury prevention, risk bearing, and the overhead cost of litigation and administration."[23] We suggest that another source of costs, namely inappropriate compensation, be added to those above. These costs are incurred whenever the compensation paid is different from the loss incurred. The inclusion of these costs is essential if we are to decide the level of protection against insolvency that is needed or to include in our analysis the costs of litigation and administration.

The costs of injuries and injury prevention—better referred to as diseases and disease prevention in our model—are straightforward from a conceptual point of view, although it might be difficult in any specific case to measure these costs. The tradeoffs between disease costs and disease prevention costs is the focal point of incentives designed to provide an appropriate level of workplace safety.

We consider the cost of risk bearing to be the costs of uncertainty that are irreducible within the system of employers, employees and insurers. Ideally, it could be measured as the irreducible disutility associated with the uncertainty. Since aggregate wealth within the system is lower in states of the world in which diseases occur, we cannot fully insure all agents within the system, as pointed out by Hirschleifer and Riley (1979). We view this as the cost of risk bearing. Quite apart from these risk-bearing costs, the cost of inappropriate compensation is viewed as the cost of misallocating contingent claims within the system. For example, if a risk-averse worker could be made just as well off (i.e., kept at the same level of expected utility) with a set of contingent claims that provided a lower expected wealth, the original set of claims can be viewed as too expensive and consequently inefficient.[24]

Assigning Liability

Even with complete information, we cannot circumvent the many problems associated with the compensating of occupational disease victims, although better information would at least help to lessen some of these problems. For example, if the source of exposure to occupational disease is clearly identifiable, perfect information about the probability of occurrence could be used to calculate compensating wage–risk premiums which in turn could be used to purchase insurance against untoward effects of the disease. If the sources of exposure are multiple, we can still assign a pro-rated liability with perfect information if the probability of occurrence is additive in the probabilities attributed to the potential sources. If the probability is not additive, the assignment of liability and/or financial responsibility among the various potential exposure sources is not so clear-cut. For example, if asbestos increases the risk of cancer five-fold and tobacco increases it ten-fold, but tobacco and asbestos taken together increase the risk of cancer 100-fold, how should we prorate the liability? Or, if three years of exposure to a particular workplace condition is considered perfectly safe, but 15 years is considered extraordinarily dangerous, how should we assign liability for a diseased worker who has worked three years for each of five such employers? Thus, we see that risk might be nonadditive across sources of exposure as well as nonadditive over time.

Epstein (1984) suggests that we assign liability in the second case to the last employer of the individual. Clearly this suggestion is aimed at reducing some of the costs of litigation and administration. If being the last in a chain of employers is random, there would not be any unfair long-run biases against a particular employer. In a sense, this is a risk-pooling scheme designed to minimize transaction costs. Unfortunately, such a scheme has adverse effects on various markets. For example, workers with a history of exposure would not be hired by new employers who would rather hire inexperienced workers with no history of exposure. The lower skill levels of such inexperienced workers affect productive efficiency as well as labor mobility.

If we wish to apportion the liability for occupational disease, the nonadditivity of effects from multiple sources is problematic. If we can determine the marginal risk introduced by a particular work environment, this would be the appropriate value to use in assigning a prorated liability. However, such a marginal contribution depends upon the risks already present and is thus sensitive to the order in which we add up the total risk. This marginal addition to risk is sensitive to personal characteristics of the worker as well as sensitive to the timing of its addition. We would not expect resulting wage–risk premiums to be paid according to each individual worker's personal characteristics, but rather to set an efficient wage–risk premium within the market and allow workers to self-select their place of employment. Only workers whose personal marginal valuation of additional job-related risk was below the market-based wage–risk premium would accept employment. If a particular exposure becomes more dangerous with a longer exposure, for example, we would expect some workers to change jobs as their marginal risk valuation surpasses the wage–risk premium over time.

If information concerning the marginal probabilities of contracting the disease from a particular exposure is used to create specific wage–risk premiums, the proper incentives for workplace safety will be instilled as is shown by Landes and Posner (1984). Landes and Posner suggest that we compensate workers who are exposed to hazards by paying them ex ante for the expected value of their future losses, which is essentially the same as paying a wage–risk premium. The risk premium is based on the additional risks faced at a particular workplace. Of course, workers who never contract the disease will be compensated anyway and workers who do contract the disease from the workplace exposure are not paid full damages. There are also workers who will develop the disease from sources not contained in the workplace. However, we cannot know for certain which workers would have developed the disease without the workplace exposure; and our ex ante liability rule based on marginal probability changes can be shown to be ex post efficient to the extent that probabilities are correctly estimated.[25]

Conclusions

Unfortunately, there are no criteria of optimality that can be generally applied when evaluating financial responsibility for occupational disease. Pareto efficiency cannot be expected and alternative models must be considered within a second-best framework. Our evaluation criteria, which are an extension of Danzon's, consider the social costs arising from five sources: injuries, injury prevention, risk bearing, overhead costs of litigation and administration, and inappropriate compensation. The incentives provided within any compensatory system play a major role in achieving (or at least striving towards) a minimization of these costs.

Asymmetry of information is of key consequence in facilitating effective compensation schemes. Incentives to reveal privately held information on the part of both employers and employees are, unfortunately, lacking. Employer-specific information concerning the particulars of workplace hazards and employee-specific information regarding exposure to contributing factors outside the workplace could be used in conjunction with each other to develop defenses against the occurrence of occupational disease. Both parties might be better off if they were to reveal their private information. However, each has an incentive to conceal private information, regardless of the other's revelation strategy, thus creating a "prisoner's-dilemma" type of situation.

If wage differentials exist to the extent that workers in riskier occupations receive a higher wage to compensate for the extra risk, these differentials could provide a perfect ex ante compensation (if information about the risk is available). If workers are further compensated after the extra risk manifests itself via the onset of an occupational disease, we would apparently have a "double dipping" into the employer's pockets by the diseased worker. An alternative view is that ex post compensation is less than complete. In this view, wage differentials compensate workers ex ante only for the difference between what they would receive with complete ex post compensation and what they can actually expect to receive ex post. If workers expect a more complete ex post compensation for occupational disease, they will require a lower compensating wage differential for a given level of risk.

A compensation mechanism for occupational disease must work well within the bounds placed upon it by imperfect information and limited resources. This chapter has considered the design of such a mechanism, paying particular attention to satisfying both ex ante and ex post criterions of efficiency. Compensation systems that are ex ante efficient—thus providing proper incentives for all economic agents to take efficient actions—cannot be deemed totally satisfactory when the system has the possibility of bankrupting itself or when ex post compensations are not correlated with damages incurred. Thus, ex post considerations must also be examined. We have defined these ex post criteria and shown how much of the existing literature has not attempted to address these issues. We see no easy answers to some of the hard issues remaining; but at least we have a framework establsihed that allows us to strive towards establishing an effective system of compensation.

Notes

1 By occupational disease we mean impairment that does not follow obviously and immediately from exposure to a work-related source. When the impairment follows immediately and obviously it will be called an accident or injury.

2 See, for example, Landes and Posner (1984), Danzon (1984), and Oi (1973).

3 See Burns and Robinson (1970).

4 See MacAvoy, Karr, and Wilson (1982), who estimate the total net worth of asbestos producers and insurers involved in the litigation at $37.1 billion while their estimate of total claims liability (in 1982) is $38.2 billion.

5 See Kakalik et al. (1983.)

6 See Viscusi (1984), p. 54.

7 The dual capacity theory allows for the injured party to sue the employer in the latter's capacity as producer of the hazardous product. Otherwise, the employer would be protected against a suit via workers' compensation laws. See, for example, Williams and Heins (1985).

8 See Viscusi (1984), p. 69; see also Tobias (1982), p. 211.

9 The concept of an occurrence is broader than that of an accident. The key distinction is that the latter is viewed as sudden and unintentional. Three Mile Island, for example, was an accident. However, a worker at another nuclear power plant might feel that she was exposed to too much radiation over her ten-year employment tenure. Such exposure would be an *occurrence*, although no *accident* had occurred.

10 See, for example, Beclake (1976).

11 For example, several deaths are caused each year by someone using chlorine bleach to help clean their toilet. When mixed with commercial toilet bowl cleaners, the bleach causes a toxic vapor to form.

12 See, for example, Selikoff (1981).

13 See, for example, the papers of Danzon (1984) and Epstein (1984) for a discussion of these problems in more detail.

14 The concept of efficiency in this setting will be discussed in the section on issues in the design of efficient compensation.

15 Epstein (1984), p. 491.

16 Viscusi (1984), p. 76, apparently overlooks this point in claiming that a penalty on past exposures "will not directly induce reductions in current risk levels. . . ." However, Viscusi is correct if no threat of penalty existed at the time of earlier noncompliance with standards of that time.

17 See Schlesinger (1983).

18 A mechanism is said to be *incentive compatible* if telling the truth is a Nash equilibrium (i.e., if all economic agents find their optimal strategy is telling the truth rather than not telling the truth). If the mechanism is also to be individually rational, meaning all economic agents would choose to participate, it cannot guarantee a Pareto-efficient outcome. See Hurwicz (1973).

19 For example, the precise location of the amputation of a body limb might need to be classified as to one of several specific locations, each with quite different scheduled awards. We also might ignore such disparities as arise from life patterns that develop years after initial exposure. Consider here the former handler of radioactive wastes who later becomes the classical pianist, only to find his hands have developed cancerous growths due to his use of defective gloves.

20 Another possibility is that a former employer has merged with or been acquired by another firm, in which case questions of liability for the new firm arise. This issue is not considered by us.

21 However, some of the programs depend on the worker's wealth status and some programs are geared towards specific diseases.

22 See Viscusi (1983).

23 Danzon (1984), p. 518.

24 This argument implicitly assumes that some economic agent, e.g., the insurer, is risk-neutral. Thus, the difference in expected wealth could be transferred to the risk-neutral agent to achieve a Pareto improvement.

25 See Landes and Posner (1984).

References

Arrow, K.J. *Social Choice and Individual Values*. New York: Wiley, 1951.

Arrow, K.J. *Essays in the Theory of Risk Bearing*. Chicago: Markham, 1971.

Barth, P.S. "A Proposal for Dealing with the Compensation of Occupational Disease." *Journal of Legal Studies* 13 (1984): 569–86.

Beclacke, M. "Asbestos Related Diseases of the Lung and Other Organs." *American Review of Respiratory Diseases* 187 (1976).

Burns, W., and D.W. Robinson. *Hearing and Noise in Industry*. London: Her Majesty's Stationery Office, 1970.

Danzon, P.M. "Tort Reform and the Role of Government in Private Insurance Markets." *Journal of Legal Studies* 13 (1984): 517–549.

Epstein, R.A. "The Legal and Insurance Dynamics of Mass Tort Litigation." *Journal of Legal Studies* 13 (1984): 475–506.

Hirshleifer, J., and J. Riley. "The Analytics of Uncertainty and Information: An Expository Survey." *Journal of Economic Literature* 17 (1979): 1375–1421.

Hurwicz, L. "The Design of Mechanisms for Resource Allocation." *American Economic Review* 68 (1973): 1–30.

Kakalik, J.S., P.A. Ebener, W.L.F. Felstiner, and M.G. Shanley. *The Cost of Asbestos Litigation.* Institute for Civil Justice, Rand Corporation, Santa Monica, CA, 1983.

Landes, W.M., and R.A. Posner. "Tort Law as a Regulatory Regime for Catastrophic Injuries." *Journal of Legal Studies* 13 (1984): 417–434.

MacAvoy, P., J. Karr, and P. Wilson. "The Economic Consequences of Asbestos-Related Diseases." Unpublished manuscript.

Oi, W. "The Economics of Producer Safety." *Bell Journal of Economics* 4 (1973): 3–28.

Rubinfeld, D.L. "On Determining the Optimal Magnitude and Length of Liability in Torts." *Journal of Legal Studies* 13 (1984): 551–563.

Schlesinger, H. "A Theoretical Model of Medical Malpractice and the Quality of Care." *Journal of Economics and Business* 35 (1983): 83–94.

Selikoff, I.J. "Disability Compensation for Asbestos-Associated Disease in the United States." Report to the U.S. Dept. of Labor, Environmental Sciences Laboratory, Mount Sinai School of Medicine, New York, NY, 1981.

Tobias, A. *The Invisible Bankers.* New York: Washington Square Press, 1982.

Viscusi, W.K. *Risk By Choice: Regulating Health and Safety in the Workplace.* Cambridge, MA: Harvard University Press, 1983.

Viscusi, W.K. "Structuring an Effective Occupational Disease Policy: Victim Compensation and Risk Regulation." *Yale Journal on Regulation* 2 (1984): 53–81.

Williams, C.A., and R.M. Heins. *Risk Management and Insurance.* 5th edition. New York: McGraw Hill, 1985.

5 EXPERIENCE RATING MATTERS

John D. Worrall
Richard J. Butler

Does the experience rating of workers' compensation insurance affect employers' provision of safety? It is possible that an experience rating system that provides some firms with other than the actuarially fair premium may result in a reduction of safety provision by some employers and a concomitant increase in job injuries. Despite the fact that one of the goals of the workers' compensation system is to provide safety incentives, there has been very little empirical evidence provided to help us answer the public policy questions about the efficacy of safety provisions. By contrast, there has been a growing body of evidence that claim frequency (Bartel and Thomas, 1982; Butler, 1983; Butler and Worrall, 1983; Chelius, 1983, 1982, 1977; Ruser, 1985; Worrall and Appel, 1982) and severity (Butler and Worrall, 1985; Worrall and Appel, 1982; Worrall and Butler, 1985) are directly related to workers' compensation benefits. Most of the claim frequency studies have focused on the risk-bearing or claim-filing behavior

We thank David Appel and Philip S. Borba for helpful comments, and the National Council on Compensation Insurance for research support. Opinions expressed in this paper are our own and are not necessarily shared by NCCI.

81

of employees. Using different specifications and time periods, these studies have provided evidence that benefit increases may raise workers' compensation costs in at least three ways: an increase in the daily cost of each claim; an increase in claim cost due to increasing claim duration; and an increase in claim frequency. With the exception of Ruser (1985), the frequency studies cited above have actually provided crude measures of the net effect of benefit changes on claim filing or injury rates. This net effect arises from countervailing forces: the employee's increased incentive for risk bearing and claims filing, and the employer's increased incentive to economize on claims. Employee effects seem to be dominating. In this chapter, we shall follow Ruser (1985) and explicitly test for both employee and employer incentives. Before we consider our empirical scheme, however, we shall briefly describe the underlying choice-theoretic model that generates the claim-filing (employee) and safety-providing (employer) behaviors.

Workers' Compensation System

Consider an economy with labor markets where employees and employers have full information and can bargain costlessly. Assume that there is perfect factor mobility and zero transaction costs. In this perfectly competitive world free of externalities, let workers be utility-of-income maximizers with income flowing from two states—an injured state and a noninjured state. Let workers be risk-averse with homogenous preferences. These workers maximize by choosing over a set of firms offering wage income (noninjured) and probability of injury pairs.

Assume that firms in this perfectly competitive world are profit maximizers and that they have different technologies. Each firm has increasing costs of injury reduction and provides safety to the point where the marginal benefit of such provision is equal to its marginal cost. Firms offering higher injury probabilities must offer a risk premium to attract workers. Firms in this economy offer profit-maximizing wage–injury probability pairs and workers choose their utility-maximizing pair. In this perfectly competitive world there is no need for government. The profit- and utility-maximizing behaviors result in an optimal provision of safety and number of injuries, and a concomitant set of risk premia or compensating differentials. If perfectly experience-rated workers' compensation insurance was introduced in this world, workers would be indifferent in choosing between purchasing their own insurance or the provision of such insurance at the actuarially fair premium (the compensating differential) via a payroll tax. Firms in this economy would continue to provide the optimal level of safety, because the cost of providing workers' compensation insurance would be exactly offset (see Dorsey, 1983) by a reduction in wage costs. This reduction in wage costs would be reflected in a reduction of the compensating *wage* differentials.

Obviously, the labor markets that we observe in the real world do not meet all of the test conditions of the theoretical world described above. For example, bargaining is costly in real labor markets. Neither employers nor workers have perfect information, and it is costly for either to acquire. In a non-Walrasian world workers cannot sort themselves costlessly across firms, and we do not know if compensating differentials fully compensate workers for risk bearing. In addition, in virtually all states the government mandates the provision of workers' compensation insurance, and it forbids many, usually smaller, firms from electing self-insurance. The experience rating program adopted by property/casualty insurers results in less than full experience rating for many firms.

Very small firms have a nominal premium price that reflects the expected accident and claims experience of all firms in the same line of business. This beginning price, called the manual rate, can be adjusted downward in response to competition. These adjustments take many forms, with the payment of dividends and price deviations on the part of insurers being two of the more common. Approximately 85 percent of firms in the United States are so small that they are not experience rated, but these firms only employ about ten percent of those who work. In 1980, a firm employing three full-time workers earning the average wage in manufacturing would probably have been experience-rated. Fifteen percent of firms, employing approximately 90 percent of those employed, are experience-rated (NCCI, 1982). The degree of experience rating varies directly with the size of the firm, the largest being fully experience-rated. The premium of the fully experience-rated firms, which is affected by market forces, reflects only their own actual (and hence expected) claims experience. Firms in between these two extreme cases (manually and fully experience-rated) have their manual rate modified based upon a weighted average of their actual and expected loss (i.e., claims cost) experience. The weight, which is zero for the actual experience of manually rated firms, and one for fully experience-rated firms, is a function of firm size. Three years of experience are used to calculate the modification factor used to adjust manual rates to reflect experience rating. As premiums vary with firm size, the safety incentive *may* vary by firm size as well.

If the reduction in wages to the firm induced by benefit increases in a world of less-than-perfect experience rating is greater than the cost of providing such benefits on the part of the firm, the marginal benefit of safety provision falls and the number of injuries could rise (see Butler and Worrall,

1983; Ehrenberg, 1984; or Ruser, 1985). Employee incentives for safety could dominate employer incentives, and the optimal number of injuries need not take place. This seems to be the principal finding of the frequency studies discussed above. However, if the fall in wages is less than the cost of providing benefits, firms have an incentive, through their increasing marginal costs of injury, to increase their level of safety provision.

Recent Research

There have been two recent empirical studies of the effect of experience rating on safety provision (Ruser, 1985; and Chelius and Smith, 1983). Ruser found statistically significant safety effects. Chelius and Smith found no measurable effects although they noted that the pattern of their results "suggests that employer behavior may not be completely random with respect to experience rating" (Chelius and Smith, 1983, p. 136).

Ruser (1985) examined the differential safety incentive by firm size. He reasoned that an increase in benefits would lower a workers' injury cost. Firms that were manually rated would *not* be able to reduce their insurance cost by engaging in the provision of additional safety. Firms that are fully experience-rated, however, can reduce their premiums because the premiums are tied directly to the firms' own, and not simply to their class, experience. Ruser maintained that he could control for the benefit level, firm size, and other variables, and test his hypothesis that larger experience-rated firms have stronger incentives to economize on injuries. His crucial test would be the sign of a firm size–benefit interaction variable. If larger firms have stronger safety incentives, this variable should have a negative sign since benefit increases should have a smaller impact on frequency rates *controlling for benefits*. Ruser used the following frequency measures per worker year as his dependent variable: all injuries; lost workday injuries; and lost workdays.

Ruser pooled cross section and time series data on 25 manufacturing industries in 41 states over the period 1972–1979. He retrieved point estimates of reduced form coefficients using a generalized least squares procedure. Ruser entered all of his variables in arithmetic form and he included both wage and production hours as right-hand-side variables. His hypothesis was sustained, since the firm size–benefit interaction variables were negative.

Chelius and Smith (1983) used a different empirical scheme. They argued that workers' behavior would be affected by benefits and not by marginal safety costs.[1] Assuming that, across states, technology within an industry was either homogeneous or varied only randomly, regulation was homogenous and worker safety incentives were similar, Chelius and Smith stipulated that experience-rated firms in the same industry should have lower injury rates than "nonexperience rated firms in the same industry in states where workers' compensation benefits are larger" (Chelius and Smith, 1983, p. 132). They tested their hypothesis using 1979 data for 15 manufacturing industries across 37 states. They regressed the difference in injury rates for plants in medium-size classes and small-size classes on average expected benefit. The benefit variable should have had a negative sign for their hypothesis to be maintained. This sign was achieved in slightly more than half of the 60 comparisons, but was only significant five times at the 0.05 level.[2]

Chelius and Smith noted the difficulty of using plants instead of firms to construct their endogenous variable. Workers' compensation prices are set at the *firm* level. Chelius and Smith knew that some of their industries consisted of a sizeable percentage of plants (perhaps over 15 percent) that were a part of larger firms. This could bias the benefit variable upward. Similarly, due to small data cells, as noted above, Chelius and Smith did not use data for the largest plant sizes. It is likely that firms with less than 1000 employees will not be fully experience-rated. Chelius and Smith also point out that firms in smaller-size classes may be partially experience-rated. As we shall see, below, both of these factors could also mitigate against finding strong negative signs on the benefit variable.

Chelius and Smith used data from a national survey, the 1976 Employer Expenditure for Employee Compensation, and found four two-digit industries that had no small plants that were parts of larger firms. They checked the signs of the benefit variables in these four industries, and for the 16 comparisons (see footnote 2) they found ten negative signs. This prompted their comment that their results may be suggestive of a nonrandom safety effect.

Model Estimation

We can use the Ruser test and our own insight on relative frequency, severity, and responsiveness to experience rating across firm size to test for experience rating effects.

Consider the current experience rating formula:[3]

$$
\text{Mod} = \frac{\begin{aligned}[\text{Actual Primary Losses} \\ + (\text{Credibility})\,(\text{Actual Excess}) \\ + (1 - \text{Credibility})\,(\text{Expected Excess Losses}) \\ + \text{Ballast}]\end{aligned}}{= \text{Total Expected Losses} + \text{Ballast}}
$$

Note that as the credibility factor goes to one, a firm is self-rated: its Mod is determined by its own experience. A firm's credibility factor will be determined by its size, the safety of its operation, the wages it pays, and the benefit structure. The first $2000 of any loss is assigned to actual primary losses and the rest to actual excess losses. The relative incentive to prevent injuries may vary with the size of the firm. For example, smaller firms with low credibility have only a small portion of excess losses (but all of their primary losses) affecting their experience modification factor. A self-rated firm feels the full effect of the excess portion. The larger firm has greater *relative* incentive to prevent excess losses.

Louise Russell (1974) used a hypothetical frequency and severity distribution to compute the elasticity of the Mod with respect to frequency and severity by firm size. She found that small firms were not very responsive with respect to severity.[4]

Although Russell did not consider the relative responsiveness, her simulations indicate that at a severity level (average claim cost) of $490, the elasticity of a firm with 500 employees is 4.1 times as great as that of a firm with 50 employees. Considering the relative responsiveness of these two firm sizes with respect to frequency at a frequency of 0.05 (the frequency level at which we compared relative severity elasticities), one finds that the elasticity of the 500-employee firm is only 2.7 times that of the 50-employee firm. More telling is the fact that although the elasticity with respect to frequency rises monotonically for *all* size classes that are less than self-rated (the percentage reduction in the Mod rises for a ten-percent reduction in the frequency as the frequency level rises), the elasticity with respect to severity *falls* monotonically over the average claim cost range Russell considered ($290 to $490) for all firms with 250 or fewer employees and *rises* for all firms with 500 or more employees.[5]

Estimating Equation

We hypothesize that

$$\text{Injury Rates} = f(\widehat{\text{Wage}}, \text{Ben}, \text{Ben Squared}, \text{Size}, \text{Size Squared},$$
$$\text{Ben-Size}, \text{Day}, \text{Race}, \text{HK}, \text{Time}).$$

All variables are defined in table 5-1.

We use a two-stage least squares procedure to retrieve point estimates of the variables' effects on the Injury Rate. For the two-stage least squares procedure, HK squared and DVAL served as the instruments, along with

Table 5-1.   Variables Used in Injury Rate and Wage Rate Equation

Dependent Variables	*Definition*
Permanent Partial	Annual injuries per employee resulting in permanent partial injuries (South Carolina Industrial Commission)
Temporary Totals	Annual injuries per employee resulting in temporary total (South Carolina Industrial Commission)
Injuries— All Indemnity Claims	The first principal component of death, permanent total, permanent partial, and temporary total rates
Wage	After-tax weekly wage of male production employees (South Carolina Department of Labor)
Independent Variables	
Ben	Expected workers' compensation benefit for the average worker
Day	Average number of days the industry was operating (South Carolina Department of Labor)
DVAL	Industry-specific measure of tightness of the product market measured as the deviation of gross sales from trend
HK	Quality-adjusted measure of human capital (real accumulated expenditure for the average worker in South Carolina, adjusted for migration and age distribution; see Butler, 1979)
Race	Ratio of black to white male production employees (South Carolina Department of Labor)
Size	Number of employees per establishment (South Carolina Department of Labor)
Time	Time Trend variable

the other exogenous variables. As our primary interest is in the injury rate regressions, we do not report the first stage (wage) results. We estimate the system for three different sets of injury rates: permanent partials, temporary totals, and an index of all indemnity claims rates. We do not have separate instruments for each of the three injury rate systems. We shall be concerned primarily with the signs of the benefit, size, and size–benefit interaction variables.

Benefit

Benefits should have a positive effect if employee incentives are dominant and a negative effect if employer incentives are dominant. Based upon the evidence from the claim frequency (or injury rate) studies cited above, we expect the sign of the benefit variable to be positive. We have included a benefit squared variable. We have no priors on its sign.

Size

A concave claims prevention function (declining marginal product of either preventing the filing of claims or accident prevention activity) implies that the coefficient of the size variable should be negative and the sign of the size squared variable should be positive.

Size–Benefit Interaction

At least three forces help to determine the sign and size of this variable:

1) Union/employee organization—in larger firms there are more unions or union-like organizations that may facilitate the filing of workers' compensation indemnity claims. The employee organization influence on the claims rate is positive (see Butler and Worrall, 1983). We attempt to partially control for this phenomenon by looking at a sample of relatively nonunionized workers. We use a sample of South Carolina industries over the period 1940–1971.

2) Monopoly power—firms that are larger *may* have more monopoly power and so be able to pass the cost of claims on to consumers. By the monopoly power argument, the contribution to the size–benefit variable's effect should be positive. We include a fixed effect for each industry to partially control for monopoly power. We can relax this control and see if the size of the size–benefit interaction variable becomes larger positive or smaller negative.

3) Experience rating effect—those firms that are larger are more likely to be experience-rated. The contribution of this influence will be negative if larger firms have stronger safety incentives as we hypothesize that they do.

We hypothesize that the net effect of these three forces will be negative, if we have successfully controlled for the first two, and that the sign of our size–benefit interaction variable will be negative. In addition we hypothesize that the size–benefit interaction will be smaller negative (or larger positive) with no industry controls, and that the negative size–benefit interaction effect will be stronger in the permanent partial runs than in the temporary total runs.

Data

The data are from information provided by the South Carolina Industrial Commission and the South Carolina Department of Labor. Cross section data on 15 industries are pooled over the 1940–1971 period. The 15 industries are listed below:

Barrels	Fertilizer	Mines
Bricks	Flour	Oil
Chemicals	Furniture	Paper
Clothing	Mattress	Printing
Electricity	Mineral	Textiles

The sample size is 468 for all of our runs.[6]

Empirical Results

The two-stage least squares results are presented in table 5-2 and elasticity estimates in table 5-3. The signs of key variables were mostly as hypothesized. The sign of the benefit variable, however, was negative in the temporary total run. Note that the first derivative was positive in the temporary total run (evaluated at the means). The benefit variable was positive in all other runs, indicating that employee incentives dominated employer incentives.

The size and size squared variables have the hypothesized sign. Evaluation of the size effect at the sample mean firm size reveals that there may be economies of size with respect to injury prevention.

The size–benefit interaction effect is negative, as hypothesized. The effect is stronger in the permanent partial run than in the temporary total run where it has the hypothesized sign but is not significant at the 0.05 level. As suggested above, we also retrieved estimated coefficients from a system of estimating equations with no industry controls. The interaction coefficients were *positive*, indicating that failure to control for an industry-fixed effect can affect point estimates significantly.

The other variables in the system performed basically as expected. Wage was negative in all runs. We expect to find an inverse relationship as the opportunity cost of an injury (the wage) rises. The day variable,

Table 5-2.[1]   Size and Benefit Effects on Claims Rates, Two-Stage Least Squares (Absolute T-Statistics)

Variable	Permanent Partial	Temporary Total	All Indemnity Claims
Intercept	−13.271	6.785	−14.857
	(1.90)	(1.14)	(.91)
Wage	−3.243*	−.154	−4.698
	(2.08)	(.11)	(1.22)
Ben	8.251	−11.139*	.907
	(1.38)	(2.20)	(.07)
Ben 2	−.667	1.683*	.589
	(.89)	(2.65)	(.34)
Size	−.513	−.419	−1.877
	(.85)	(.82)	(1.34)
Size 2	.170*	.082*	.380*
	(4.57)	(2.59)	(4.37)
Size-Ben	−.350*	−.093	−.541
	(1.86)	(0.58)	(1.23)
Day	.271	.833*	1.476
	(.65)	(2.34)	(1.51)
Race	.311	.415*	.965*
	(1.52)	(2.39)	(2.02)
HK	.505	1.018	1.726
	(1.85)	)4.39)	(2.71)
Time	.020	−.1050*	−.083
	(.57)	(3.55)	(1.01)
R2	.748	.815	.803
F (regr)	54.64*	81.44*	75.21*
F (ben/size)	.800	4.486*	5.583*

1. Included dummy variables as industry controls.

Table 5-3.   Injury Rate Elasticities

With Respect To	Permanent Partials	Temporary Totals	All Indemnity Claims
Benefits	2.457	0.16	1.985
Firm size	−0.495	−0.155	−1.017

included to capture the effect of production intensity, was positive, i.e., the injury rate rises with production intensity. The injury rate rises with the proportion of black workers employed. We have found this result in other samples (see Worrall and Butler, 1983). The human capital variable was positive. We expect this variable to be negative with more educated workers bearing less risk, all else constant.

Conclusions

Our findings conform with those of Ruser. Although we estimate structural equations and use a different sample and time period, we find that experience rating matters. We find that the effect is stronger for more serious cases. It is worth noting that a firm size variable, such as that used by Ruser and by us, is an imperfect proxy for experience rating. We cannot differentiate between firms that self-insure and those that insure with property/casualty insurers. There is evidence that firms that elect insurance with property/casualty insurers can have stronger safety incentives (see Victor, 1985). To the extent that very large firms that self-insure *have less* of a safety incentive than firms that are experience-rated, óur inability to control for self-insurance mitigates against finding a negative sign (an employer effect), and the incentives for safety provision inherent in the workers' compensation experience rating plan may be *stronger* than those we report in our results. Similarly, if smaller firms have greater relative incentive to control frequency, the coefficient in temporary total runs can be damped down.

Consider that permanent partial claims can account for 60 percent or more of the cost of indemnity claims. These claims are more likely to find their way into the actual excess loss component of the Mod. Firms will carry these losses for three years (with a one-year lag) for purposes of calculating their Mod. Given Victor's (1985) simulation findings, we would expect to find greater elasticities for the size–benefit interaction in the runs for more serious claims. This is what we observed in our results. The elasticity was 0.093 for temporary total, 0.350 for permanent partial, and 0.541 for all indemnity claims. The all indemnity claims rate includes the death and permanent totals claims. In other words, a ten-percent increase in the size–benefit interaction variable, all else constant, would result in a 5.41-percent decrease in the indemnity claims rate.

The results presented in table 5-3 are instructive. The benefit elasticity, calculated at the means, is huge. A ten-percent increase in real benefits results in a 24.57-percent increase in the permanent partial injury rate and a 19.85-percent increase in the indemnity claims rate. These benefit utilization factors would lead to large cost increases. Similarly, the injury rate elasticities with respect to firm size, calculated at the means, are large. A ten-percent increase in firm size leads to a 4.95-percent decrease in the permanent partial injury rate and a 10.17-percent reduction in the all indemnity claims rate.

There are several caveats concerning these resutls that deserve special mention. We have pooled cross section time series data for a single state and 15 industries over a period that preceded the National Commission on State Compensation Laws. We were also able to use closed claims only. We found that the ratio of open to closed claims was fairly stable over the sample period, however. Although there is a need for a study of the experience rating effect that controls for the impact of self-insurance and uses microdata at the firm level, the preliminary evidence from Ruser's study and from our two studies (see also chapter 2) is in. Experience rating matters.

Notes

1 If there are wage–benefit tradeoffs, (or wage–workers' compensation tradeoffs), this assumption may be difficult to buy. However, it is no more tenuous than assuming that wage is exogenous, or that the reduced form can be modeled with a linear specification.

2 The comparisons were over four plant sizes: (500–999 workers) versus (1–19 workers); (500–999) versus (20–49); (250–499 workers) versus (1–19 workers); and (240–499 workers) versus (20–49 workers); and the 15 two-digit SIC industries.

3 For a full explanation of the National Council on Compensation Insurance Experience Rating Plan, see NCCI (1982). For an introduction to the Plan, see NCCI (1981). For an explanation of the formula as we present it here, see Victor (1985).

4 See her tables 1 and 2, p. 367.

5 The elasticity is 1.0 for self-rated firms for both severity and elasticity in her tables. One of the implications of Victor's (1985) research is that the elasticity of 1.0 could be reached at less than full experience rating.

6 The loss of 12 observations is due to mergers and to nonreporting by some industries after 1969. For a discussion of the sample, see Butler (1983).

References

Bartel, Ann P., and Glenn Thomas Lacy. "OSHA Enforcement Industrial Compliance, and Workplace Injuries." Working Paper No. 953. Cambridge, MA: National Bureau of Economic Research, 1982.

Butler, Richard J. "Black/White Wage and Employment Changes: A Look at

Production Workers in South Carolina, 1940–1971." Unpublished Ph.D. Dissertation, University of Chicago, 1979.

Butler, Richard J. "Wage and Injury Rate Response to Shifting Levels of Workers' Compensation." In John D. Worrall (ed.), *Safety and the Workforce: Incentives and Disincentives in Workers' Compensation*. Ithaca, NY: ILR Press, 1983.

Bulter, Richard J., and John D. Worrall. "Work Injurry Compensation and the Duration of Nonwork Spells." *Economic Journal*, September 1985.

Butler, Richard J., and John D. Worrall. "Workers' Compensation: Benefit and Injury Claim Rates in the Seventies." *Review of Economics and Statistics* 65, 4 (1983): 580–589.

Chelius, James R. "Workers' Compensation and the Incentive to Prevent Injuries." In John D. Worrall (ed.), *Safety and the Workforce: Incentives and Disincentives in Workers' Compensation*. Ithaca, NY: ILR Press, 1983.

Chelius, James R. "The Influence of Workers' Compensation on Safety Incentives." *Industrial and Labor Relations Review* 35 (1982): 235–242.

Chelius, James R. *Workplace Safety and Health*. Washington D.C.: American Enterprise Institute, 1977.

Chelius, James R. and Robert S. Smith. "Experience Rating and Injury Prevention." In John D. Worrall (ed.), *Safety and the Workforce: Incentives and Disincentives in Workers' Compensation*. Ithaca, NY: ILR Press, 1983.

Dorsey, Stuart. "Employment Hazards and Fringe Benefits: Further Tests for Compensating Differentials." In John D. Worrall (ed.), *Safety and the Workforce: Incentives and Disincentives in Workers' Compensation*. Ithaca, NY: ILR Press, 1983.

Ehrenberg, Ronald G. "Workers' Compensation, Wages and Risk of Injury." A paper presented at the Conference on New Perspectives on Workers' Compensation, ILR School, Cornell University, Ithaca, NY, Oct. 16, 1984.

National Council on Compensation Insurance. *The ABC's of Experience Rating*. New York: NCCI, 1981.

National Council on Compensation Insurance. *An Indepth View of Experience Rating*. New York: NCCI, 1982.

Ruser, John W. "Workers' Compensation Insurance, Experience Rating and Evaluation. U.S. Bur. Of Labor Statistics, Washington, D.C., 1984 (mimeo).

Russell, Louise B. "Safety Incentives in Workmen's Compensation Insurance." *The Journal of Human Resource* 9 (Summer 1974): 361–375.

Victor, Richard B. "Experience Rating and Workplace Safety." In John D. Worrall and David Appel (eds.), *Benefit Issues in Wokers' Compensation: Adequacy, Equity and Efficiency*. Ithaca, NY: ILR Press, 1985.

Worrall, John D. "Compensation Costs, Injury Rates and the Labor Market." In John D. Worrall (ed.), *Safety and the Labor Force: Incentives and Disincentives in Workers' Compensation*. Ithaca, NY: ILR Press, 1983.

Worrall, John D., and David Appel. "Some Benefit Issues in Workers' Compensation." In John D. Worrall and David Appel (eds.), *Benefit Issues in Workers' Compensation: Adequacy, Equity and Efficiency*. Ithaca, NY: ILR Press, 1985.

Worrall, John D., and David Appel. "The Wage Replacement Rate and Benefit Utilization in Workers' Compensation Insurance." *Journal of Risk and Insurance* 49, 3 (1982): 361–371.

Worrall, John D., and Richard J. Butler. "Workers' Compensation: Benefits and Duration of Claims." In John D. Worrall and David Appel, eds., *Workers' Compensation Benefits: Adequacy, Equity and Efficiency*. Ithaca, NY: ILR Press, 1985.

Worrall, John D., and Richard J. Butler. "Health Conditions and Job Hazards: Union and Nonunion Jobs." *Journal of Labor Research* 4 (1983): 339–347.

6 THE RELATIONSHIP BETWEEN STANDARD PREMIUM LOSS RATIOS AND FIRM SIZE IN WORKERS' COMPENSATION INSURANCE

Scott E. Harrington

The National Council on Compensation Insurance (NCCI) prospective experience rating plan is used in workers' compensation pricing in a large majority of states. This plan commonly is applied to about 15 percent of employers, and approximately 90 percent of the labor force may be employed by these firms. The NCCI plan adjusts an individual employer's manual premium based on its own loss experience during a three-year experience period to produce the standard premium for the firm. In principle, this process is designed to produce expected standard premium loss ratios for each class of employment that will equal the NCCI target for a state, which is called the standard permissible loss ratio. The standard premiums then are subject to premium discounts and the addition of an expense constant to incorporate differences in insurer expenses for firms of different sizes.[1] Hence, loss ratios based on net premiums, i.e., standard premiums adjusted by premium discounts and the expense constant, are expected to decline with increases in firm size.

Thanks are due Philip Borba and David Durbin for providing the data used in this study and for answering numerous questions concerning workers' compensation insurance rate-making procedures.

95

The accuracy of the administered pricing process in terms of producing premiums equal to expected costs may have important distributional and allocative consequences. Even if premiums equal expected costs in aggregate for a given industry class and over all classes, deviations between premiums and expected costs across firms in a given industry class would affect the distribution of wealth and firm-specific decisions with regard to loss control. With regard to the experience rating plan, it has long been known that the objective of such a plan should be to produce standard loss ratios that do not differ among identifiable subgroups of firms in a given industry class (e.g., Perryman, 1937). On the other hand, it also has long been known that large employers tend to have lower loss ratios, at least in terms of manual premiums, than small employers (e.g., Perryman, 1937; Kallop, 1975; and NCCI, 1982). Because of this phenomenon, the application of experience rating generally produces a total amount of standard premiums that is less than the total amount of manual premiums. Manual rates are adjusted for the so-called "off-balance" so that the overall level of standard premiums will be sufficient to achieve the loss ratio objective.

As will be described more fully later, the NCCI experience rating plan cannot be expected to produce ratios of expected losses to *standard premiums* that are invariant with respect to firm size if expected losses per unit of exposure in an industry tend to decline with increases in firm size, despite the fact that the weight given to a firm's own loss experience increases with firm size. Analysis of the extent to which standard loss ratios vary according to firm size is made difficult because of (1) likely heterogeneity in any relationship between losses and firm size across industries and states, (2) the lack of credibility of losses for small firms, and (3) the potential nonnormality of workers' compensation loss distributions for firms of any size, which tends to impede hypothesis testing. Nevertheless, analysis of this issue would be important for a number of reasons. At a minimum, evidence that loss ratios vary according to firm size would raise the question of whether the overall pricing program produces rates that differ systematically from expected losses according to firm size. The findings also might be helpful in evaluating the validity of claims that the experience rating plan may be unfair to either small or large employers.

The objective of this chapter is to provide empirical evidence of the extent to which standard loss ratios vary according to firm size under the NCCI experience rating plan. Aggregate data for the three broad industrial groupings defined by the NCCI plan are analyzed for four different states. The overall empirical results suggest that standard loss ratios generally were negatively related to average payroll of the firms studied.

We first illustrate that standard loss ratios will tend to vary with firm size if the expected loss per exposure varies with firm size, and we briefly discuss implications of this result for equity and efficiency. We then describe the data and methodology used to examine the relationship between standard loss ratios and firm size. The empirical results are presented next. Finally, we offer conclusions and suggestions for further work.

Expected Loss Ratios Under the NCCI Plan

Let S denote a firm's payroll in $100 units and r denote the expected loss rate under the NCCI plan. For simplicity, it is assumed that r and S are constant over time and that r equals the true average expected loss per unit of payroll in the firm's industry class (i.e., issues of loss development, loss limitations, law amendments, and trend are ignored). Let M denote the experience modification factor and P the standard premium.

Given these assumptions and notation, the standard premium for a firm can be written $P = MrS/k$ where k, a constant for each firm in the industry, is a factor ($k < 1$) to account for expenses, profit, and any adjustment for off-balance. The actual expected loss for a firm can be written $\bar{L} = (1 + d)rS$, where d is the proportionate deviation of the firm's expected loss rate from the industry average, which is assumed to be constant over time.

The experience modification factor is given by

$$M = [A_p + WA_e + (1 - W)E_e + B]/[E + B] \qquad (6.1)$$

where A_p is the firm's actual primary losses, A_e is the firm's actual excess losses, E_e is the firm's expected excess losses, and E is the firm's expected total losses (all aggregated for the entire experience period).[2] W is the credibility factor for actual excess losses and B is the ballast factor.[3]

Let D denote the D-ratio, i.e., the expected ratio of primary expected losses (E_p) to total expected losses (E) for the industry, so that $E_p = DE$ and $E_e = (1 - D)E$.[4] Assume that D also equals the expected ratio of primary to excess losses for the individual firm, so that the firm's expected primary losses during the experience rating period equal $(1 + d)DE$ and its expected excess losses equal $(1 + d)(1 - D)E$.[5] Substituting the firm's expected primary and expected excess losses for A_p and A_e, respectively, and $(1 - D)E$ for E_e, the expected value of M can be written

$$\bar{M} = \{(1 + d)[DE + W(1 - D)E] + (1 - W)(1 - D)E + B\}/(E + B). \qquad (6.2)$$

Upon simplification, this can be written

$$\bar{M} = 1 + dQ \tag{6.3}$$

where

$$Q = [D + (1 - D)W]/(1 + B/E). \tag{6.4}$$

It can easily be shown that Q is greater than zero for any firm subject to experience rating, that it increases with S, and that it achieves a maximum value of one for a self-rated firm.[6] The fact that Q is less than one unless the firm is large enough to be self-rated illustrates the fact that experience rating is necessarily imperfect. Firms with higher or lower expected loss rates than the average for their industry class are only partially rewarded or penalized by the experience modification factor.

Substituting for M in the formula for the firm's standard premium, the expected value of the firm's standard premium equals

$$\bar{P} = (1 + dQ)rS/k. \tag{6.5}$$

Define R as the probability limit of the firm's standard loss ratio, i.e., $R = \bar{L}/\bar{P}$. Then R can be written

$$R = k(1 + d)/(1 + dQ). \tag{6.6}$$

Since k is constant across firms, variation in R only will reflect variation in d and Q. Q increases with firm size (i.e., with S), and the average value of d is zero. Differentiating R with respect to S would indicate the relationship between expected standard loss ratios and firm size. However, without detailed knowledge of the relationship between d and S, the sign of this derivative is ambiguous.[7] Nonetheless, if small firms were to have values of d greater than zero and large firms were to have values of d less than zero on average, R would tend to be greater for small firms.[8]

There are at least two reasons that d might be expected to decline with firm size in an industry. First, there may be increasing returns to scale in the production of safety. Second, the experience rating plan itself may provide greater financial incentive to large firms for investment in safety than to small firms. While there has been some dispute about the magnitude of the incentive effects of experience rating (e.g., Russell, 1974; Victor, 1982; and Chelius and Smith, 1983), there is evidence that injury rates tend to decline with increases in the number of employees, at least beyond some minimum number of employees (e.g., Butler, 1983).[9]

If standard loss ratios were to vary systematically with firm size, a number of questions would arise. One would be whether other components of the pricing program, specifically the expense program, might operate so as to mitigate any errors in the experience component of the premium. If not, the impact of such errors could conceivably create availability problems if they produced inadequate premiums for certain (presumably small) firms. Alternatively, net premiums might still be of sufficient magnitude to ensure availability of coverage to all firms provided that the statewide standard permissible loss ratio contained enough "fat" so that the higher standard loss ratios for some firms would not entail economic losses for insurers. In other words, net premiums might be sufficient to cover expected costs for all firms with any excess that varied according to firm size competed away by service, dividends, or both according to the relationship between expected losses and firm size. However, even if availability problems were not produced, the question would arise as to whether efficiency could be improved by formally considering the relationship between expected losses and firm size in the pricing process, assuming that such consideration would be technically feasible.

Methodology and Data

The data set analyzed, which was supplied by the NCCI, included total standard earned premiums, actual losses, the number of firms, and total payroll for firms in 16 standard premium ranges for each of the three broad industry groupings (manufacturing, construction, and all other) for four states.[10] The standard permissible loss ratio for each state also was supplied. The premium ranges (shown in table 6-1) were chosen to provide a reasonable balance between the number of firms and total expected losses in each category. The states, policy periods, standard permissible loss ratios (SPLRs), and actual statewide loss ratios (ALRs) for the experience-rated firms are listed below:[11]

State	Period	SPLR	ALR
Georgia	1980–1981	.642	.504
Indiana	1982–1983	.6496	.676
Kansas	1980–1981	.6142	.521
Virginia	1982–1983	.6706	.407

Using these data, the ratio of actual to expected losses (A/E) was calculated for each premium category for each industry grouping by dividing actual losses by the product of the SPLR and total standard earned premiums.[12] Hence, these ratios will exceed (be less than) one if the actual loss ratio for a category exceeds (is less than) the SPLR.

Table 6-1.   Number of Times A/E Exceeds Industry Value by Premium Category

Premium Range (1000s)	Georgia	Indiana	Kansas	Virginia	Total
$1–$2	2	3	2	2	9
$2–$3	1	2	0	1	4
$3–$4	2	1	3	1	7
$4–$5	1	2	1	2	6
$5–$6	2	1	3	2	8
$6–$7	1	1	1	3	6
$7–$8	1	2	1	1	5
$8–$9	1	1	2	3	7
$9–$10	3	3	1	0	7
$10–$12.5	2	2	2	2	8
$12.5–$15	1	1	2	2	6
$15–$25	1	1	3	0	5
$25–$35	1	2	2	2	7
$35–$50	0	1	0	1	2
$50–$100	2	1	0	1	4
>$100	1	1	0	0	2

Note: There are three comparisons for each state and a total of 12 for the four states combined.

The A/E ratios obviously reflect a considerable degree of aggregation. The NCCI classification scheme includes over 600 separate industry classes. Analysis of class-specific data at the state level would be plagued by severe credibility problems. If a general tendency exists for standard loss ratios to vary in the same direction in relation to firm size for many classes, analysis of the aggregate data may be able to provide evidence of this effect. Moreover, there would appear to be no a priori reason to expect that aggregation across classes would be likely to bias the analysis towards finding a relationship between standard loss ratios and firm size.

Two general procedures were employed to investigate the relationship between the A/E ratios and firm size. The first involved comparing each value of A/E to the corresponding overall value for the broad industry grouping in the state. If standard loss ratios tend to be higher for small firms than for large firms, the values for the small premium categories should tend to exceed the industry value and vice versa for the large premium categories. This procedure is likely to be fairly weak in detecting systematic relationships in view of the large degree of random noise in the A/E values.

The second procedure involved the use of weighted least squares regression methods to estimate the relationship between the A/E values and the average payroll per firm in each category.[13] Four different models were estimated for each state to allow for alternative functional forms.[14]

Model 1—Linear:

$$A/E = a + bS + e.$$

Model 2—Exponential:

$$A/E = \exp(a + bS + e).$$

Model 3—Quadratic:

$$A/E = a + bS + cS^2 + e.$$

Model 4—Box–Cox flexible functional form:

$$(A/E^\lambda - 1)/\lambda = a + bS + e.$$

S is average payroll per firm (in \$1,000,000s) in each premium category, and e is a statistical disturbance that is assumed to have mean zero and variance proportional to total expected losses (the product of SPLR and standard earned premiums) for each premium category.

Model 1 is a simple linear model. Model 2 allows for a nonlinear but monotonic relationship between A/E and S.[15] Model 3 allows a quadratic and thus nonmonotonic relationship between A/E and S. Model 4 transforms A/E using the power transformation suggested by Box and Cox (1964). The transformation parameter, λ, is estimated along with a and b. Hence, model 4 allows the data to determine the functional form. When $\lambda = 1$, model 4 is equivalent to model 1. When $\lambda = 0$, it is equivalent to model 2.

Models 1, 2, and 3 were estimated using weighted least squares based on the assumed proportional relationship between the variance of e and total expected losses.[16] Model 4 was estimated using weighted least squares for λ values from $-.5$ to 1.5 in steps of $.1$ and then choosing the value of λ that maximized the log-likelihood for the model under the assumption that e is normally distributed with variance proportional to total expected losses.[17]

The models first were estimated separately for each state using pooled data for the three industry groupings, yielding a total of 48 observations (16 premium categories for each industry grouping). Standardized residuals were calculated and tested for departures from normality using the skewness statistic, the kurtosis statistic, and a test based on the maximum absolute standardized residual.[18] These tests should provide rough evidence of whether standard tests of statistical significance can be expected to provide useful information. In addition to the pooled runs, models 1, 2, and 3 were estimated separately for each industry grouping to allow for parameter heterogeneity. The resultant samples included 16 observations for each state.

Empirical Results

The number of times that A/E for each premium category exceeded the industry values of A/E is shown in table 6-1 for each state and for all states combined. As noted, these comparisons may be of limited value because of the random variation in standard loss ratios. The results in table 6-1 do not provide any strong evidence of a monotonic relationship between standard loss ratios and firm size. However, the results in the "total" column for the smallest premium range and for two of the three largest ranges would appear to be at least weakly consistent with a negative relationship between standard loss ratios and firm size.

Estimation results for the alternative A/E models for the pooled data are shown in table 6-2. Except for Virginia, the results provide evidence of a negative and statistically significant relationship between the A/E ratios and average payroll. For models 1, 2, and 4, the t-values for the coefficient on the average payroll variable indicate a negative and highly significant relationship.[19] The F-statistics for testing the hypothesis that $b = c = 0$ in model 3 also would be highly significant if the disturbances were normally distributed.

Again with the exception of Virginia, the kurtosis statistics and maximum absolute standardized residuals do not reject the normality hypothesis. However, the skewness statistics indicate significant positive skewness at the .05 level for the quadratic model for Indiana and Kansas and for the linear model for Indiana. The values of the skewness statistic for the linear model for Kansas and the Box–Cox model for Indiana also are close to the .05 critical value (.55). The exponential model shows little evidence of positive skewness or other indication of nonnormality. With the exception of the skewness statistic for Indiana, the results for the Box–Cox residuals also would appear to be consistent with the normality hypothesis. The overall results for Georgia, Indiana, and Kansas suggest that the significant relationship implied by the t-values and F-statistics is unlikely to be attributable to nonnormal errors.

Based on a likelihood ratio test, the hypothesis that $\lambda = 1$ would be rejected at the .10 level (but not the .05 level) for Indiana and Kansas (and

Table 6-2. Estimation Results for Alternative *A/E* Models: Pooled Data

Model	Statistic	Georgia	Indiana	Kansas	Virginia
1. Linear	b	−.015	−.016	−.024	−.009
	$t(b)$	−3.190	−4.198	−4.038	−.922
	S	.461	.919*	.516	1.459*
	K	.002	.467	−.021	3.819*
	U	2.649	2.854	2.778	4.255*
2. Exponential	b	−.019	−.019	−.030	−.005
	$t(b)$	−3.302	−5.395	−4.377	−.323
	S	.090	.207	−.417	−1.040*
	K	−.116	.447	.446	2.770*
	U	2.591	2.769	2.700	3.886*
3. Quadratic	$b \times 10$	.004	.020	−.554	−1.090
	$\hat{c} \times 10$	−.013	−.007	.022	.071
	F(2,45)	5.374	9.954	8.599	2.270
	S	.300	.925*	.553*	1.505*
	K	−.148	.608	−.027	4.634*
	U	2.642	2.939	2.711	4.208*
4. Box−Cox	b	−.017	−.018	−.027	−.007
	$t(b)$	−3.281	−4.939	−4.307	−.547
	$\hat{\lambda}$	.300	.400	.400	.300
	S	.196	.522	.003	−.125
	K	−.121	−.027	−.056	.493
	U	2.621	2.670	2.359	2.738

Note: S denotes skewness, K denotes kurtosis, and U denotes the maximum absolute value of the standardized residuals from the weighted regressions.
* normality of standardized residuals is rejected at .05 level.

at the .01 level for Virginia). The hypothesis that $\lambda = 0$ would not be rejected for any of the states (except Virginia). In general, models 1, 2 and 4 support the conclusion of a negative relationship between the A/E ratios and average payroll. For model 3, the high correlation between average payroll and average payroll squared led to large standard errors for the estimated coefficients. As a result, conclusions about whether the relationship is monotonic cannot be made.

With regard to the results for Virginia, the normality tests indicate very poorly behaved residuals for each model except model 4. The estimated coefficients on the average payroll variable are negative in models 1, 2, and 4, but the absolute *t*-values are small. Two observations appeared to be substantial outliers based on the magnitude of their standardized residuals (one positive and one negative).[20] Deleting these observa-

Table 6-3. Estimated Coefficients and *t*-values for Average Payroll Variable by Industry Group: Exponential Model

Industry	Georgia	Indiana	Kansas	Virginia
Manufacturing	−.051	.011	−.015	−.209
	(2.79)	(1.36)	(.37)	(.85)
Construction	.015	−.031	−.041	−.086
	(.59)	(4.52)	(.47)	(.85)
All Other	−.013	−.020	−.031	−.007
	(1.65)	(5.81)	(5.03)	(.41)

Note: The samples include 16 observations. Parameter homogeneity across industry groups rejected by F-test at .10 level for Indiana only. Absolute *t*-values are in parentheses.

tions reduced the evidence of nonnormality, but had little impact on the estimated coefficients.

Based on an F-test (which, of course, assumes normality of the disturbances), the hypothesis that the parameters of each model (both intercepts and slopes) were the same for each industry grouping would be rejected at the .10 level for Indiana for models 1 and 2 and for Georgia for model 3.[21] The estimated coefficients and *t*-values for the average payroll variable that were obtained when model 2 was estimated separately for each industry grouping are shown in table 6-3. The results for model 1 were quite similar. As can be seen in table 6-3, the estimates vary considerably across industries and states. Nonetheless, ten of the 12 values are less than zero. If the distributions of the disturbances in each case were symmetric, the probability of observing this number of negative values due to chance alone would be about .02. While the evidence of skewness suggests that this probability may be understated, the results shown in table 6-3 generally support the hypothesis that A/E ratios tend to decline with increases in average payroll.

Conclusions

The NCCI experience rating plan cannot be expected to produce standard loss ratios that are invariant with respect to firm size if expected losses vary according to firm size. The empirical results of this study suggest that the standard loss ratios for three of the four states examined were negatively and significantly related to average payroll. This result would be expected if expected losses decline with firm size, at least beyond some minimum scale of operations for some industry classes.

It would be desirable to conduct additional analyses of the relationship between standard loss ratios and firm size for other states and time periods to determine whether the findings of this study reflect a general phenomenon. Analysis of the relationship for specific industry classes also would be desirable. Credibility problems associated with industry-specific analysis might be reduced to tolerable levels if data can be efficiently pooled across time, states, or both. Further work also should consider direct estimation of the relationship between losses and payroll for specific industries, again assuming that credibility problems can somehow be managed. The question of economies of scope, as well as scale, for multi-industry firms conceivably might be considered.

Research in these areas might provide a basis for refining the workers' compensation pricing process to consider formally the effect of firm size on expected losses, perhaps by letting the expected loss rate depend on firm size. Refinements of this type could be especially important to insurers in states that either have adopted or will be adopting competitive rating for workers' compensation insurance.

Notes

1 For detailed descriptions of the experience rating and expense programs, see NCCI, *An In-Depth View of Experience Rating* and *Workers' Compensation Expense Program*.

2 Primary losses include the entire amount of each claim less than or equal to $2000. For claims greater than $2000, the amount included in primary losses equals the loss times $10,000 divided by the loss plus $8000, subject to a maximum of $10,000. As a result of this procedure, the amount included in primary losses increases at a decreasing rate as claim size increases. Excess losses equal total losses less primary losses. See NCCI (1982).

3 Credibility values range from zero for risks with expected losses less than or equal to $25,000 to one for risks with expected losses greater than or equal to $830,000. The ballast factor equals $(1 - W) \times \$20,000$. This factor is included to reduce fluctuations in M caused by anomalies in an employer's loss experience.

4 The D-ratio used in practice varies across industry classes but is constant within each industry class. It is estimated using past data on primary and excess losses. For further discussion, see NCCI (1982).

5 If the true value of D varies across firms, then a firm's expected standard loss ratio also would reflect such variation in addition to any impact of size on d. In particular, if D is increasing in firm size, then the relationship between the expected loss ratio and firm size that is suggest below would be mitigated, if not eliminated.

6 $W = 1$ and $B = 0$ for a self-rated firm.

7 Let y_x denote the partial derivative of y with respect to x. The sign of R_S equals the sign of $d_S(1 + dQ) - (d_SQ + dQ_S)(1 + d)$.

8 For example, assume that $d = .1$ for small firms and $-.1$ for large firms and that the respective values of Q for small and large firms are .1 and .5. Then R would equal $1.09k$ for the small firms and $.95k$ for the large firms.

9 Also see Russell's (1974) discussion of the evidence presented by the National Commission on State Workmen's Compensation Laws.

10 The data did not include experience for firms that were smaller than the experience rating eligibility threshold. The data included experience for firms that were not yet eligible for experience rating because they had fewer than three years experience.

11 The actual losses were developed for 18 months. The standard permissible loss ratios, which are on an ultimate basis, were used to calculate rates during the policy period. They were divided by 1.13 to eliminate the margin for loss adjustment expenses. Data also were supplied for the premium range $0–$1000. These data were excluded due to the inability to adjust for loss constants that are charged to firms whose premiums inclusive of the loss constant would be less than $500. Data were combined for the ranges $50,000–$75,000 and $75,000–$100,000 because the construction industry grouping for Virginia had no firms in the latter category.

12 The standard earned premium data supplied by the NCCI included the sum of the expense constants for the firms in each category. This sum was deducted by the author prior to calculating the expected losses for each category.

13 Similar results were obtained using both the average expected loss per firm in each category and the midpoint of each premium category ($150,000 was used for the greater-than-$100,000 category).

14 Model specific subscripts on the parameters and disturbance terms are omitted for convenience.

15 Taking the log of both sides of model 2 gives $\log A/E = a + bS + e$, which is linear in the parameters. Preliminary analysis with a log-linear model (i.e., $\log A/E = a + b(\log S) + e$) produced results that were similar to those for model 2.

16 Similar results were obtained using weights based on total payroll.

17 Estimation of the Box–Cox model under heteroscedasticity is described by Lahiri and Egy (1981).

18 The last test is described by Lund (1975). He also tabulates estimated upper bounds for the critical values for this test. The results of the skewness and kurtosis tests will only be approximate, given that the standardized residuals are not independent. Industry and premium category dummies were not included in the pooled models to allow for nonzero covariances across observations. Preliminary analysis involving the regression of A/E on such dummies provided virtually no evidence of significant fixed effects for the industry and premium categories.

19 Spitzer (1984) has criticized the use of t-values to test for significance in Box–Cox models because they will not be invariant to the unit of measurement for the dependent variable. However, likelihood ratio tests of the hypothesis that $b = 0$ (which were conditional on the estimated value of λ) produced significance levels similar to those implied by the t-values for model 4.

20 The observations were for the greater-than-$100,000 premium range for manufacturing (negative residual) and for the $2000–$3000 range for construction (positive residual).

21 Likelihood ratio tests of parameter homogeneity were not conducted for model 4.

References

Box, G., and D. Cox. "An Analysis of Transformations." *Journal of the Royal Statistical Society B* 26 (1964): 211–243.

Butler, R. "Wage and Injury Rate Response to Shifting Levels of Workers' Compensation." In J. Worrall, (ed.), *Safety and the Work Force*. Ithaca, NY: ILR Press, 1983.

Chelius, J., and R. Smith. "Experience Rating and Injury Prevention." In J. Worrall, (ed.), *Safety and the Work Force*. Ithaca, NY: ILR Press, 1983.

Kallop, R. "A Current Look at Workers' Compensation Ratemaking." *Proceedings of the Casualty Actuarial Society* 61 (1975): 62–133.

Lahiri, K., and D. Egy. "Joint Estimation and Testing for Functional Form and Heteroskedasticity." *Journal of Econometrics* 15 (1981): 299–307.

Lund, R. "Tables for an Approximate Test for Outliers in Linear Models." *Technometrics* 17 (1975): 473–476.

National Council on Compensation Insurance. *An In-Depth View of Experience Rating*. New York: NCCI, 1982.

National Council on Compensation Insurance. *Workers' Compensation Expense Program*. New York: NCCI.

Perryman, F. "Experience Rating Plan Credibilities." *Proceedings of the Casualty Actuarial Society* 24 (1937): 60–125.

Russell, L. "Safety Incentives in Workmen's Compensation Insurance." *Journal of Human Resources* 9 (1974): 361–375.

Spitzer, J. "Variance Estimates in Models With the Box–Cox Transformation." *Review of Economics and Statistics* 66 (1984): 645–652.

Victor. R. *Workers' Compensation and Workplace Safety*. Santa Monica, CA: Rand Corporation, 1982.

7 THE IMPACT OF OPEN COMPETITION IN MICHIGAN ON THE EMPLOYERS' COSTS OF WORKERS' COMPENSATION

H. Allan Hunt
Alan B. Krueger
John F. Burton, Jr.

Private insurance carriers sell workers' compensation insurance in all but six states and now account nationally for about 60 percent of all benefit payments.[1] Traditionally, the procedure used to determine workers' compensation insurance rates limited the amount of price competition among carriers. Recently, however, several states have changed their laws or regulations to permit more competition in rates. This study examines in detail the impact on the employers' costs of workers' compensation insurance as a result of the January 1, 1983 introduction of open competition in Michigan.

The paper provides extensive data on the employers' costs of workers' compensation in Michigan for 1983, 1984 and 1985 (three full years of experience under open competition). To measure the impact of open com-

We express our appreciation to Barry Llewellyn of the National Council on Compensation Insurance (NCCI), Roy Stewart and Jon Heikkinen of the Compensation Advisory Organization of Michigan (CAOM), and Jean Carlson, Kevin Clinton, Bob Klein, and Laura Appel of the Insurance Bureau of the State of Michigan for their assistance. We also benefited from comments by David Appel and Philip Borba on an earlier version of this chapter.

petition, actual premium costs in these years are compared to simulated costs developed using the earlier rate-making procedures. Between 1980 and 1983 Michigan adopted a number of other statutory changes relating to benefits and procedures that were designed to lower workers' compensation costs. Therefore, additional data on workers' compensation costs in Michigan and some comparison states are provided for 1978 and 1984 in order to determine whether the substantial rate reductions in Michigan were simply the result of broad industry trends rather than the result of the impact of open competition. The paper also reviews the limited data available for other open competition states in 1984 to determine whether the Michigan experience may be reproducible in other states.

In December 1980, the National Association of Insurance Commissioners adopted a model competitive rating bill that suggested a new rate-making procedure for all voluntary property/casualty insurance lines. It endorsed the concept of using market forces to assist in "regulating" the price of insurance in workers' compensation programs as well. This proposal seems to have struck a responsive chord in workers' compensation because of the general impression that carriers had little chance to compete in terms of price at the beginning of the policy period using traditional rate adjustments, such as experience modification and premium discounts.[2] This is not to say that there was no competition; carriers were always free to compete in service to the policyholder, premium payment plans, dividends, and other such devices. Furthermore, the threat of the self-insurance option for large firms clearly acted as a constraint on insurance pricing behavior.

However, in many jurisdictions it is now increasingly possible for private carriers to compete for business by varying the insurance rates at the beginning of the policy period. The variations in some instances are made for groups of employers and sometimes even for individual employers. Table 7-1 provides information on three types of competitive devices that have been adopted in those states with private insurance carriers: open competition, rate deviations, and schedule rating.

The desirability and causes for this increased ability of carriers to compete on an ex ante basis have been widely discussed and will not be repeated here.[3] Indeed, because the movement towards competition has been so recent, only limited information is available about the extent of the competition and the impact of the various competitive devices on workers' compensation costs. We concentrate on assessing the impact of open competition on workers' compensation costs in Michigan.

This paper relies on data provided by the National Council on Compensation Insurance (NCCI), by the Compensation Advisory Organization of Michigan (CAOM), and by the Insurance Bureau of the State of Michigan. It also relies on other earlier work by the authors, particularly the study conducted for the Governor's Special Counselor on Workers' Compensation, Prof. Theodore St. Antoine.[4] That study provided a comparison of workers' compensation rates in 47 jurisdictions as of January 1, 1984. We have extended the Michigan data in this paper through 1985, but the sections of this chapter that rely on interstate comparisons utilize the 1984 data. Before turning to an in-depth examination of the data for Michigan, we provide an overview of competitive devices and their probable impact.

Competitive Devices

Open Competition

The most drastic change in the pricing mechanism has occurred in those states with open competition (also referred to as competitive rating). In such states, carriers may charge whatever insurance rates they feel are appropriate. Carriers are required to file their rates with the state insurance department, but some states do not even require prior approval before using these rates.

There are differences among the open competition states, including whether a rating bureau (usually renamed data service organization) will publish advisory rates and, if so, what those rates can include. As shown in table 7-1, there were nine states with open competition laws in effect by 1984. In Arkansas, Georgia, Illinois, Rhode Island, and Vermont, the advisory rates contain both pure premium (covering expected losses) and an expense loading; these rates are comparable to manual rates in states without open competition. In Kentucky, Oregon, and Minnesota the published rates contain only pure premium. In Michigan, the published rates cover pure premium plus loss adjustment expenses, but exclude the trend factor.

Unfortunately, there are only limited data showing the actual impact of open competition on the employers' costs of workers' compensation. This is not surprising, since the earliest open competition law only went into effect in Arkansas in June of 1981 and the other eight states with open competition laws have accumulated even less experience under these procedures. However, because of some unique data that have been collected

Table 7-1. Ability of Private Carriers to Modify Insurance Rates on an Ex Ante Basis as of January 1, 1984

	Open Competition		Status of Rate Adherence Agreements and Deviations			Schedule Rating
	Status	Effective Date	Status	Number of Companies	Impact on Rate Level	Type
Alabama			X	6	0.1	U
Alaska			X	4	0.8	I
Arizona			X	64	16.8	U
Arkansas	O	6/17/81	No			
California						U
Colorado			NP	23	19.1	
Connecticut			NP	81	7.2	
Delaware (1)			X	14	1.3	I
District of Columbia			X	8	0.1	U
Florida			X	125	7.3	
Georgia	O	1/1/84				
Hawaii			X	N.A.	N.A.	
Idaho	O	8/18/82	X	2	1.0	
Illinois			X	N.A.	N.A.	
Indiana			X	82	4.8	
Iowa			X	82	3.3	
Kansas			X	49	2.4	
Kentucky	O	7/15/82	X	49	2.4	
Louisiana			X	3	0.2	
Maine			X			
Maryland			X	93	6.2	
Massachusetts			No			
Michigan	O	1/1/83				
Minnesota	O	1/1/84				

State						
Mississippi		X	0	0		U
Missouri		X	91	3.9		U
Montana		NP	14	17.1		I
Nebraska		X	67	4.4		
New Hampshire		X	41	4.0		
New Jersey		No				
New Mexico		X	11	0.2		U
New York		X	68	2.5		
North Carolina		X	97	9.0		
Oklahoma		X	40	1.6		
Oregon	O	7/1/82	X			
Pennsylvania (1)		X	108	7.8		
Rhode Island	O	9/1/82	X			U
South Carolina		X	9	0.1		U
South Dakota		X	9	0.5		U
Tennessee		X	61	3.2		U
Texas		No				
Utah		X	22	14.2		U
Vermont	(O)	7/1/84	X	23	3.2	
Virginia		X	83	4.4		
Wisconsin		No				

O denotes presence of open competition
(O) denotes that open competition became effective after January 1, 1984
X denotes deviations permitted
NP denotes rate adherence agreements not permitted
I denotes individual schedule rating
U denotes uniform schedule rating

Source: Derived from *Workers' Compensation Rating Laws—A Digest of Changes*, NCCI, 1982, with quarterly updates thru October, 1984; C. Arthur Williams, Jr., "Workers' Compensation Insurance Rates: Their Determination and Regulation, A Regional Perspective," manuscript presented at the First Annual Conference on Workers' Compensation, Rutgers University, May 9–10, 1983; correspondence from Barry I. Llewellyn, Assistant Secretary, NCCI, letter, June 26, 1984.

(1) The data for Delaware and Pennsylvania were provided in correspondence from Stephen S. Makgill, President, Pennsylvania Compensation Rating Bureau, letter, September 7, 1984.

in Michigan, a reasonably accurate assessment can be made now of the initial impact of open competition in that state.

Deviations

The second type of competitive device included in table 7-1 is rate deviations.[5] (A similar device—a prohibition on rate adherence agreements—is also shown in table 7-1). In some of the states in which rating organizations publish manual rates, individual carriers are permitted to deviate from the published rates after securing the insurance commissioner's approval. The crucial differences from open competition are that prior approval of the deviations are required, while in open competition such approval may not be required, and that the deviations offered by a particular carrier are generally uniform for all policy holders in the state, while in open competition no such uniformity is necessary.

For most states the NCCI provided information on the impact of deviations on the insurance rates in 1984. The data in table 7-1 are incomplete because the National Council has only limited information on deviations in states with independent rating organizations. Additional information derived from the recent paper by Williams (1986) has been added to the table. The table indicates that, in general, the impact of rate deviations is small overall. However, the states of Arizona, Colorado, Montana, and Utah show considerable cost reductions due to rate deviations.

Schedule Rating

The third type of competitive device catalogued in table 7-1 is schedule rating. Schedule rating plans have been introduced in many jurisdictions in recent years. Under these plans, insurers can change (usually decrease) the insurance rate the employer would otherwise pay through credits (or debits) based on an evaluation of subjective factors, such as the employer's loss-control program, that might affect the cost of carrying the risk. Such credits can also be used as a marketing tool in order to reduce premiums to meet competition.[6]

There are two types of schedule rating. In states with uniform schedule rating plans, the regulators permit all carriers to use the proposed schedule rating plan. If all carriers are not given this permission, then individual carriers can apply for approval of their schedule rating plans. Unfortunately, virtually no data were available about the impact of schedule rating plans on the employers' costs of workers' compensation when the cost estimates for 47 states as of 1984 were prepared.[7]

The Possible Consequences of These Competitive Devices

One view of workers' compensation is that prior to open competition and the other competitive devices listed in table 7-1, the use of dividends, retro-spective rating, and so forth had squeezed all excess profits and unnecessary expenses out of workers' compensation insurance.[8] If this is true, then arguably the only result of open competition will be to reduce insurance rates at the beginning of the policy period with a corresponding reduction in dividends (or other postpremium payments) at the end of the policy period. This view amounts to saying that open competition has no impact at all on the employers' costs of workers' compensation.

The other view of workers' compensation insurance is that prior to the use of open competition and the other competitive devices discussed here, excess profits or unnecessary administrative expenses existed in workers' compensation insurance, and that competition has the potential to eliminate or reduce these expenses, thereby lowering the costs of workers' compensation to employers. It is to test these alternative hypotheses that we now examine the impact of open competition in Michigan.

Open Competition in Michigan

The cost of doing business in Michigan came under severe scrutiny in the late 1970s, led by reactions to what legislators regarded as runaway workers' compensation costs.[9] Repeated efforts to amend the workers' compensation statute in Michigan had run into labor opposition, but the momentum provided by business climate fears and changes in the political balance of power finally broke through the roadblocks in 1980 and 1981.[10] In addition to a number of benefit changes, the package of reforms included an aggressive attack on the insurance rate-making system in Michigan.

First, a mandatory insurance rate reduction of at least 20 percent was imposed for policies written in 1982. Second, Public Acts 7 and 8 of 1982 abolished the old system of administered pricing and implemented a new open competitive rating system in its place. The purposes of these structural changes were stated as follows:

(a) To protect policyholders and the public against the adverse effects of excessive, inadequate, and unfairly discriminatory rates.

(b) To promote price competition among insurers writing workers' compensation insurance so as to encourage the lowest possible rates consistent with benefits and with maintaining the solvency of insurers.

(c) To provide regulatory controls and other activity in the absence of competition.

(d) To improve the availability, fairness and reliability of workers' compensation insurance.[11]

The state moved aggressively to deregulate workers' compensation rate-making by implementing open competition with no transition period on January 1, 1983. Insurers were required to file rates individually; bureau rate filings were prohibited. The old rating bureau was replaced by a new system of a Data Collection Agency (which included representatives of the general public and employers) overseeing a Designated Advisory Organization that would collect and disseminate pure premium data (i.e. data on losses only);* no advisory manual rates were allowed. Further, the Insurance Commissioner was required to certify annually that a workable level of competition existed within the workers' compensation insurance market in the state or further remedial options would be triggered.[12]

It was clear that legislators in Michigan wanted wholesale changes in the way workers' compensation insurance was priced in the state. Furthermore, it was apparent that a majority felt that excess profits existed in the workers' compensation line, and that the imposition of open competition would reduce the costs of workers' compensation for Michigan employers, without materially reducing benefits for injured workers.

One of the fortuitous results of open competition in Michigan is that the reorganized rating bureau (called the Compensation Advisory Organization of Michigan, or CAOM) began to accumulate new data to document the actual cost of workers' compensation insurance to Michigan employers. As a result of this initiative, Michigan has the best data currently available to make a preliminary assessment of the impact of open competition on workers' compensation insurance costs.[13]

Table 7-2 presents aggregate data on the workers' compensation market in Michigan for 1982 through 1985. Open competition was effective in Michigan on January 1, 1983, so the table reports the last year of administered pricing (including the effects of the mandated reduction in manual premiums in 1982) and the first three years of open competition. It is apparent that there was an immediate and dramatic reduction in workers' compensation insurance costs in Michigan in 1983.[14] The average rate for voluntary policies declined from $2.47 in 1982 to $2.15 in 1983, a reduction of 13.0 percent on top of the 22.0 percent reduction from the last rate filing

Table 7-2. Policies, Premium, and Payroll: 1982–1985

	Year	Policies	Premiums* (000's)	Payroll (000's)	Average Rate** (Per $100)
Voluntary	1982	120,097	$589,283	$23,833,497	$2.47
Market	1983	126,310	572,079	26,648,607	2.15
	1984	138,641	507,312	26,450,110	1.92
	1985	135,902	550,444	26,547,392	2.07
Placement	1982	12,290	$20,686	$ 614,531	$3.37
Facility	1983	10,383	17,932	424,748	4.22
	1984	10,478	16,305	404,271	4.03
	1985	15,313	50,205	1,279,062	3.93
Total	1982	132,387	$609,969	$24,448,028	$2.50
	1983	136,693	590,011	27,073,355	2.18
	1984	149,119	523,617	26,854,381	1.95
	1985	151,215	600,649	27,826,454	2.16

 * 1982–1983: Standard premium obtained from unit statistical reports.
  1984–1985: Total estimated annual premium obtained from policy declarations.
 ** Premiums/(Payroll/100)
 Source of Data: Compensation Advisory Organization of Michigan.

under administered pricing in 1982.[15] The exhibit shows an additional decline of 10.7 percent from 1983 to 1984. Further, these rate reductions were accomplished along with a net reduction in the size of the placement facility (assigned risk policies) over this period. This suggests that insurance was readily available, despite the substantial price reductions.

The exhibit shows that both trends were reversed in 1985, however. The average rate increased by 7.8 percent from 1984 to 1985 in the voluntary market and, more worrisome, the number of employers who were forced into the assigned risk pool (at substantially higher rates) increased by over 46 percent. Still, the exhibit shows that after three years of experience there was a gross reduction of 13.6 percent in the average cost of workers' compensation insurance in Michigan.[16]

These gross impacts can hide more than they reveal, however, since they do not control for changes in the distribution of payroll among classifications. Thus, if manufacturing classifications (or other high-cost classifications) were increasing (decreasing) in importance over this period, the gross impact figures would underestimate (overestimate) the true impact. Such employment trends would not be suprising, given that 1982 was the trough of the worst recession in Michigan since the Great Depression.

Table 7-3. Components of the Employers' Costs of Workers' Compensation Insurance in Jurisdictions without Open Competition

	1. Pure Premiums
×	2. Loading Factors
=	3. Manual Rates
×	4. Payroll
=	5. Manual Premium without Constants
+	6. Expense Constant (and Loss Constant)
=	7. Manual Premium with Constants
×	8. Experience Rating Modification
=	9. Standard Earned Premium
−	10. Adjustment for Premium Discount and Retrospective Rating
=	11. Net Earned Premium
−	12. Dividends to Policyholders
=	13. Net Cost to Policyholders
÷	14. Payroll
=	15. High Adjusted Manual Rates

Layoffs of up to one-third of production workers in Michigan were not unusual at the time.

In order to determine the net impact of open competition due to factors other than changing employment patterns, we employed the methodology previously developed by Burton to measure the interstate differences in the employers' costs of workers' compensation insurance. The method, described in detail in Burton and Krueger (1986), has been modified for the present study in order to determine the impact of open competition on Michigan workers' compensation insurance costs in 1983, 1984, and 1985.

The procedure uses insurance rates for 71 insurance classes that account for 73 percent of national payroll, or the 70 Michigan classes than encompass the 71 classes used for most jurisdictions.[17] We present results using both national weights for these classes and Michigan weights based on payroll in the state during the individual year being examined;[18] the analysis in this section primarily relies on the results using Michigan weights.

The insurance costs for the 71 classes are compared using what is in effect the 15-step procedure shown in table 7-3, although in practice some of the steps are combined. The actual costs in Michigan under open competition are determined by a simpler procedure, but in order to compare these actual costs with the insurance costs that would have prevailed if open competition had not been adopted, the 15-step procedure must be used.

Pure premiums are the only insurance rates published in Michigan since 1983; they represent the loss and loss adjustment costs per $100 of payroll. The normal *loading factors* not included in the Michigan pure premiums include the trend factor and allowances for profits and expenses other than loss adjustment expenses. Had Michigan used the normal loading factors, pure premiums would have been increased by 53.9 percent (1983), 55.4 percent (1984), or 47.2 percent (1985) to produce *manual rates*.[19] These simulated manual rates are shown in tables 7-4 and 7-5, line (1). Prior to 1983, Michigan published equivalent manual rates; most states still do.

Manual rates multiplied by *payroll* produces *manual premium without constants*; this figure plus the *expense constant* (and formerly the loss constant) produces *manual premium with constant*. An expense constant of $35 is used for Michigan for 1983–1985 since this was the figure in use before open competition;[20] the estimated impact is to increase manual premium by a factor of 1.012.

Manual premium is adjusted for some employers on the basis of their own experience; the result of applying the *experience rating modification* is *standard earned premium*. The national data showing the impact of experience rating are in panel A of table 7-6; equivalent data for Michigan are in panel B.

Standard earned premium as modified for many employers by the *adjustment for premium discounts* (for quantity purchases) and *retrospective rating* (a type of experience rating) for the remainder, is *net earned premium*. National data on the adjustments are in panel A of table 7-7, with equivalent Michigan data in panel B.

The final significant reduction for many employers in their workers' compensation costs is the payment of *dividends*, which when subtracted from *net earned premium* results is the *net cost to policyholders*. National data on dividends are presented in panel A of table 7-8, with Michigan data in panel B.

The *net cost to policyholders* can be divided by *payroll* to produced *high adjusted manual rates*, which are the net costs of workers' compensation insurance per $100 or payroll. High adjusted manual rates are the insurance costs actually paid by employers in the absence of open competition, deviations, or schedule rating. *Simulated high adjusted manual rates* are our estimates of what employers would have paid in Michigan after 1983 if these competitive devices were not present.

Three variants of simulated high adjusted manual rates for 1983, 1984, and 1985 are shown in line (2) of tables 7-4 and 7-5; the variants represent three estimates of the appropriate differential between steps 3 and 15 of table 7-3.[21] The three variants never differ by more than 3.5 percent in

Table 7-4. Michigan Workers' Compensation Insurance Rates, 1983–1985 (Using Michigan Payroll Weights for 70 Insurance Classifications)

	1983 Variants			1984 Variants			1985 Variants		
	I	II	III	I	II	III	I	II	III
(1) Average Costs of Manual Rates (Simulated)	2.557	2.557	2.557	2.337	2.337	2.337	2.031	2.031	2.031
(2) Average Costs of High Adjusted Manual Rates (Simulated)	2.015	2.015	1.951	1.842	1.865	1.807	1.600	1.672	1.621
(3) Average Manual Rates in Actual Transactions	1.985	1.985	1.985	1.816	1.816	1.816	1.836	1.836	1.836
(4) Average Charged Rates in Actual Transactions	1.695	1.695	1.695	1.477	1.477	1.477	1.610	1.610	1.610
(5) Low Adjusted Manual Rates after Impact of Dividends	1.497	1.497	1.497	1.284	1.284	1.284	1.439	1.439	1.439
(6) Gross Impact of Open Competition ((1)-(5))/(1)	41.5%	41.5%	41.5%	45.1%	45.1%	45.1%	29.1%	29.1%	29.1%
(7) Net Impact of Open Competition ((2)-(5))/(2)	25.7%	25.7%	23.3%	30.3%	31.2%	28.9%	10.1%	13.9%	11.2%

Table 7-5. Michigan Workers' Compensation Insurance Rates, 1983–1985 (Using National Payroll Weights for 71 Insurance Classifications)

	1983 Variants			1984 Variants			1985 Variants		
	I	II	III	I	II	III	I	II	III
(1) Average Costs of Manual Rates (Simulated)	3.045	3.045	3.045	2.902	2.902	2.902	2.601	2.601	2.601
(2) Average Costs of High Adjusted Manual Rates (Simulated)	2.400	2.400	2.323	2.287	2.316	2.243	2.050	2.141	2.076
(3) Average Manual Rates in Actual Transactions	2.347	2.347	2.347	2.223	2.223	2.223	2.293	2.293	2.293
(4) Average Charged Rates in Actual Transactions	2.016	2.016	2.016	1.814	1.814	1.814	1.982	1.982	1.982
(5) Low Adjusted Manual Rates after Impact of Dividends	1.780	1.780	1.780	1.576	1.576	1.576	1.772	1.772	1.772
(6) Gross Impact of Open Competition ((1)−(5))/(1)	41.5%	41.5%	41.5%	45.7%	45.7%	45.7%	31.9%	31.9%	31.9%
(7) Net Impact of Open Competition ((2)−(5))/(2)	25.8%	25.8%	23.4%	31.1%	32.0%	29.7%	13.6%	17.2%	14.6%

121

Table 7-6. Ratio of Standard Earned Premium to Manual Premium (All Amounts in Thousands)

Year	Standard Earned Premium (includes constants)	Manual Premium (includes constants)	Ratio of Standard to Manual Premium	
			Average (one year)	Average (three years)
		Panel A: National Data		
1979–1980	9,926,353	9,955,666	0.997	—
1980–1981	9,785,572	9,877,404	0.991	—
1981–1982	10,205,035	10,259,779	0.995	0.994
1982–1983	9,057,274	9,204,430	0.984	0.990
		Panel B: Michigan Data		
1979–1980	967,598	972,460	0.995	—
1980–1981	968,486	1,014,202	0.955	—
1981–1982	763,636	782,421	0.976	0.975
1982–1983	625,097	642,274	0.973	0.967

Source: National Council on Compensation Insurance, Exhibits on Earned and Manual Premium Ratios.

Table 7-7. Ratio of Net Earned Premium to Standard Earned Premium, All Carriers (All Amounts in Thousands)

Year	Standard Earned Premium	Return to Policyholders	Net Earned Premium	Ratio of Net to Standard Premium	
				Average (one year)	Average (three years)
			Panel A: National Data		
1979	15,328,627	1,506,943	13,821,684	0.902	—
1980	17,305,936	2,139,464	15,166,472	0.876	—
1981	17,445,572	2,056,360	15,389,212	0.882	0.886
1982	16,980,825	2,213,084	14,767,741	0.870	0.876
1983	16,674,457	1,766,007	14,908,450	0.894	0.882
1984	17,490,153	1,281,874	16,208,279	0.927	0.897
1985	19,504,411	1,225,927	18,278,484	0.937	0.920
			Panel B: Michigan Data		
1979	985,728	117,989	867,739	0.880	—
1980	1,026,665	166,667	859,998	0.838	—
1981	954,776	130,791	823,985	0.863	0.860
1982	747,520	154,745	592,775	0.793	0.834
1983	625,398	115,424	509,974	0.815	0.828
1984	380,076	Not applicable	368,415	—	—

Sources: Panel A: National Council on Compensation Insurance (NCCI), Insurance Expense Exhibit (Countrywide) for individual years 1979–1985; Panel B: NCCI, Results of National Council's Calendar Year Call for Workers' Compensation Experience for individual years 1979–84.

Note: *Michigan data from different years are not comparable. For example, 1983 data on standard premium are at company rate level; 1984 data are standard earned pure premium.

123

Table 7-8. Ratios of Dividends and Net Cost to Net Earned Premium (All Amounts in Thousands)

Year	Net Earned Premium	Dividends	Net Cost to Policyholders	Ratio of Dividends to Net Earned Premium		Ratio of Net Cost to Net Earned Premium	
				Average (one year)	Average (three years)	Average (one year)	Average (three years)
			Panel A: National Data				
1979	13,821,683	1,022,619	12,799,064	0.074	—	0.926	—
1980	15,166,472	1,351,289	13,815,183	0.089	—	0.911	—
1981	15,389,212	1,497,031	13,892,181	0.097	0.087	0.903	0.913
1982	14,767,741	1,692,745	13,074,996	0.115	0.100	0.885	0.900
1983	14,908,450	1,690,198	13,218,252	0.113	0.108	0.887	0.892
1984	16,208,394	1,733,950	14,474,444	0.107	0.112	0.893	0.888
1985	18,278,484	1,837,540	16,440,944	0.101	0.107	0.899	0.893
			Panel B: Michigan Data				
1979	914,323	51,522	862,801	0.056	—	0.944	—
1980	905,529	62,892	842,637	0.069	—	0.931	—
1981	859,599	74,548	785,051	0.087	0.071	0.913	0.929
1982	619,403	85,085	534,318	0.137	0.093	0.863	0.907
1983	533,323	74,903	458,420	0.140	0.117	0.860	0.883
1984	555,228	63,085	492,143	0.114	0.131	0.886	0.869
1985	681,800	49,148	632,652	0.072	0.106	0.928	0.894

Sources: Panel A: National Council on Compensation Insurance, Insurance Expense Exhibit (Countrywide) for individual years 1979–1985; Panel B: Michigan Department of Licensing and Regulation/Insurance Bureau, "By-Line Statistical Report—Workers' Compensation," (calendar years 1979–1985).

any year; however, there is variation among the years as to which variants produce the largest and smallest differentials between manual rates and high adjusted manual rates.

Variant I uses the three-year average of Michigan workers' compensation experience for the period immediately before the introduction of competitive devices (including deviations) into the state. As previously described, an expense constant of $35 is used, which increases manual premium by a figure of 1.012, a figure used for all three variants shown in tables 7-4 and 7-5. Table 7-6, panel B shows that the impact of experience rating during policy years 1979–1980 to 1981–1982 was to make standard earned premium equal to 0.975 times manual premium. Table 7-7, panel B indicates that net earned premium was 0.860 times standard earned premium in 1979–1981. Table 7-8, panel B demonstrates that the net cost to policyholders was 0.929 times net earned premium in 1979–1981. The overall differential between manual rates and high adjusted manual rates in variant I is 1.012 (step 6 of table 7-3) times 0.975 (step 8) times 0.860 (step 10) times 0.929 (step 12), which equals 0.788. Thus, prior to the introduction of deviations and open competition into Michigan beginning in 1982, high adjusted manual rates were 78.8 percent of manual rates. Variant I assumes that the 78.8 percent relationship is appropriate for adjusting the simulated manual rates for Michigan in 1983–1985 in order to determine what high adjusted manual rates would have been in these recent years if competitive devices had not been introduced into Michigan.

Variant II uses the three-year average of recent national experience to estimate the appropriate relationship for 1983–1985 between simulated manual rates and simulated high adjusted manual rates in Michigan. Thus for 1983, the national experience during policy years 1980–1981 to 1982–1983 with experience rating was to make standard earned premium equal to manual premium times 0.990 (table 7-6, panel A); for 1981–1983, standard earned premium times 0.882 equals net earned premium (table 7-7, panel A); and net earned premium times 0.892 equals net cost to policyholders (table 7-8, panel A). Chain-multiplying these factors as well as the 1.012 impact of the Michigan expense constant produces an overall factor of 0.788. Thus Variant II produces simulated high adjusted manual rates for 1983 that are 78.8 percent of the simulated manual rates for that year (by coincidence the same figure produced by Variant I). Similar calculations produce percentages of 79.8 percent for 1984 and 82.3 percent for 1985.[22] Variant II, in effect, assumes that the relationships in Michigan in 1983–1985 between simulated manual rates and simulated high adjusted manual rates would have been identical to the national relationships during those years if Michigan had not used any type of competitive pricing during those years.

Variant III blends Michigan and national experience to produce estimates of simulated high adjusted manual rates. For the three years prior to
the introduction of competitive devices into Michigan, net costs to policyholders were 77.9 percent of manual premiums with constants in the state.[23]
The corresponding national figure for the same years was 80.4 percent,
indicating that prior to the introduction of competitive devices into Michigan, the differential between manual rates and high adjusted manual rates
was about 2.5 percent greater in Michigan than nationally. Variant III
takes the Variant II estimates for 1983–1985 (which are based solely on
national data) and assumes that Michigan's 2.5 percent "excess" differential between manual rates and high adjusted manual rates would have
persisted into recent years if competition had not been introduced into the
state. Variant III thus produces a differential of 76.3 percent for 1983, 77.3
percent for 1984, and 79.8 percent for 1985.

Lines (1) and (2) of table 7-4 and 7-5 represent our estimates of the
manual rates that would have been promulgated in Michigan in 1983–1985
if traditional rate-making procedures had continued and if competitive
devices (including schedule rating) had not been introduced. Obviously the
high adjusted manual rates (line (2)) depend on assumptions about what
would have happened to premium discounts, dividends, and so forth if
these competitive devices had not been permitted, but the three variants
represent what we believe are a reasonable range of assumptions.

Lines (3) to (5) of table 7-4 and 7-5 provide information on the actual
costs of workers' compensation in Michigan during 1983–1985. The Compensation Advisory Organization of Michigan (CAOM) provided the data
in lines (3) and (4), which are derived from the "Information Pages" that
each carrier must file for each workers' compensation policy sold in the
state. Under open competition, the initial charges offered to employers
will vary among carriers. The average manual rates charged by carriers in
actual transactions with employers during 1983–1985 are shown in line (3).
The data indicate that under open competition, the manual rates charged
by carriers are considerably less than the manual rates that would have
been charged using the rate-making procedures in place before open competition. (This can be seen by comparing lines (1) and (3) of tables 7-4
and 7-5.)

Under open competition in Michigan, carriers are also able to compete
by using different experience rating formulas, expense and loss constants,
and premium discounts than those used in states without open competition.
The insurance rates actually charged to employers in Michigan during 1983–
1985 after these factors are shown in line (4) of tables 7-4 and 7-5.

There are two additional adjustments to manual rates that are not reflected in line (4) of tables 7-4 and 7-5. The principal factor not accounted

for is dividends paid after the expiration of the policies. The alternative to dividends for some larger employers are retrospective rating plans. Unfortunately, the cost impact of retrospective rating cannot be measured in Michigan.[24]

If open competition is driving down the initial rates charged to employers (manual rates) and also leading to competition in terms of premium discounts, experience rating, and similar factors, then reducing dividends is an obvious way for carriers to adjust their overall charges for workers' compensation insurance if the rates prior to open competition were not higher than necessary to cover losses and administrative expenses.

It is difficult to reach a definitive judgement about the impact of open competition on dividends in Michigan because dividends typically are paid on the basis of experience with policies from previous years and because the latest data on Michigan dividends pertain to 1985, as shown in table 7-8, panel B. The absolute amount of dividends peaked in 1982 and has declined steadily since that time. However, dividends as a percentage of premiums increased every year from 1979 to 1983 when measured on an individual year basis and increased from 1981 to 1984 when dividends are compared to premiums over three years.

In 1985, however, dividends dropped substantially on both an absolute and relative basis. It is still too early to be confident about the ultimate impact of open competition on dividends in Michigan, but the evidence suggests that dividends have begun to respond to price decreases. For 1983, the three-year average of dividends as a percentage of premiums was 11.7 percent. This 11.7 percent was used to reduce the average charged rates for 1983 shown in line (4) of tables 7-4 and 7-5 to produce the low adjusted manual rates after estimated impact of dividends shown in line (5). A similar procedure was used for the 1984 rates shown in tables 7-4 and 7-5, where the low adjusted manual rates in line (5) are 13.1 percent lower than the average charged rates shown in lines (4). For 1985, the low adjusted manual rates are 10.6 percent lower than the average charged rates.

The low adjusted manual rates shown in line (5) of table 7-4 are our best estimates of what the 70 types of Michigan employers actually paid for workers' compensation insurance in 1983–1985, considering all the consequences of open competition, such as carrier decisions on manual rates, experience rating formulae, and dividends. These actual charges are substantially less than the simulated manual rates shown in line (1) of the table, which represent our estimates of the manual rates that would have been promulgated if open competition had not been adopted in Michigan and if manual rates had been established by use of the procedures traditionally utilized by the National Council on Compensation Insurance and the Workers' Compensation Rating and Inspection Association of Michigan.

Line (6) of table 7-4 indicates, for example, that for 1983–1985 the low adjusted manual rates in line (5) were from 29.1 to 45.1 percent below the simulated manual rates shown in line (1).

It would be inappropriate, however, to attribute all of the differences shown in line (6) to open competition, since even in the absence of open competition (or the other competitive devices discussed earlier), most Michigan employers would have paid insurance rates less than manual rates because of premium discounts, dividends, etc. Our best estimates of what Michigan employers would actually have paid in 1983–1985 if open competition had not been adopted (or these other recently introduced competitive devices were not available) are shown as the simulated high adjusted manual rates in line (2) of table 7-4.

The estimated net impact of open competition is the difference between these high adjuated manual rates (line (2)) and the low adjusted manual rates (line (5)). The percentage estimates of net impact of open competition are shown in line (7) of tables 7-4 and 7-5. Depending on the variant used, the estimates in table 7-4 using Michigan payroll weights range from 23.3 to 25.7 percent for 1983, from 28.9 to 31.2 percent for 1984, and from 10.1 to 13.9 percent in 1985. Equivalent estimates in table 7-5 using national payroll weights are from 23.4 to 25.8 percent in 1983, from 29.7 to 32.0 percent in 1984, and from 13.6 to 17.2 percent in 1985.

Thus the net impact of open competition on workers' compensation costs for Michigan employers in 1983–1985 was substantially greater than the impact shown in the aggregate figures of table 7–2, according to our best estimates. We stress that this finding must be used with caution. One reason, as discussed earlier, is that more time is needed before the ultimate impact of open competition on dividends can be determined. The substantial dividends shown in table 7-8, panel B may continue to dissipate with time. Also, the initial result of open competition may be to induce a degree of competition among carriers that cannot be sustained over time.

Arguably, carriers are engaged in a form of predatory price-cutting that will jeopardize some carriers' financial solvency and ultimately will lead to more realistic (or sustainable) and higher rates. More time will be needed to assess the permanent consequences of open competition on workers' compensation insurance rates, but the erosion of apparent savings from 1984 to 1985 is very problematical. Between 1984 and 1985, simulated high adjusted manual rates (line (2) of tables 7-4 and 7-5) decreased, but average charged rates in actual transactions increased (line (4)), which helps explain why the apparent net impact of open competition declined in the last year. One reason is that the improving claims experience of recent years is entering the actuarial data base. For instance, there was a reduction in the trend factor (utilized in deriving simulated manual rates from pure premiums) from 13.6 to 6.9 percent between 1984 and 1985.

Obviously the exact value for the net impact of open competition is sensitive to the assumptions made about what would have happened to manual rates in 1983–1985 if the old administered pricing system had been maintained. No one can say for sure what would have happened, but it is very impressive that these net impacts followed the 22 percent reduction already imposed on administered prices in 1982. The estimates for the net impact in 1983, 1984, and 1985 fall in a range of ten to 30 percent. Whatever the specific assumptions, it is difficult to imagine that this magnitude of price reduction is an illusion.

In addition, a recent review of the impact of open competition in Michigan from a regulatory point of view has been provided by Robert Klein (1986). Klein examined changes in workers' compensation insurance market shares, concentration ratios, market entry and exit data, trends in loss ratios, testimony on availability, and more. His findings include the following: (1) market concentration ratios slightly increased from 1982 to 1985; (2) no significant trend toward either entry or exit of carriers occurred in the Michigan market; (3) availability problems were increasing as indicated by employers having difficulty finding carriers willing to take their business; (4) substantial price variations existed in the Michigan workers' compensation insurance market; (5) large price reductions took place through mid-1984, followed by increases in the latter half of 1984 and throughout 1985; (6) significant increases occured in the loss ratios for workers' compensation insurance in Michigan after 1982; (7) solvency problems among carriers did not perceptibly increase. Klein concludes (at pp. 106–07):

> Aside from the current availability problems, all indications suggest that competitive rating has worked very well in Michigan. There is no evidence that, on the whole, employers have been hurt by competitive rating. Rather, it appears that competitive rating has significantly lowered the cost of workers' compensation insurance for employers.

The next section examines more closely the decline in workers' compensation rates in Michigan up to 1984, both by comparing it to trends in other states and by delving into the actuarial data more thoroughly, in order to validate the results in this section.

Changes Between 1978 and 1984 in Michigan Workers' Compensation Costs

We have seen that workers' compensation costs came down rapidly in 1983 and 1984 in Michigan. But if these same trends were typical of other states'

Table 7-9. Workers' Compensation Costs in Michigan Relative to National Average and Other Great Lakes States Average, 1958–1984: Adjusted Manual Rates for 44 Classes

	1958	1962	1965	1972	1975	1978	1984
(1) Michigan	.450	.694	.715	.914	1.238	1.890	1.267
(2) U.S. Average (28 states)	.618	.711	.791	.783	1.019	1.420	1.368
(3) Ratio Michigan to U.S. ((1)/(2))	.728	.976	.904	1.167	1.215	1.331	.926
(4) Seven Other Great Lakes States Average	.514	.577	.600	.648	.871	1.275	1.063
(5) Ratio Michigan to Other Great Lakes States ((1)/(4))	.875	1.203	1.192	1.410	1.421	1.482	1.192

Average for Other Great Lakes States is a six-states average for 1958–1965; New York data not available prior to 1972.

experience, we may incorrectly be ascribing the influence of the normal underwriting cycle to the imposition of open competition in Michigan. Thus an important question is the extent to which Michigan's workers' compensation costs were improving relative to other states during the period in question. Fortunately, directly comparable workers' compensation cost data are available for 1978 and 1984. Thus, it is possible to answer the question of relative cost trends directly to further confirm our estimates of the net impact of open competition on workers' compensation insurance costs in Michigan.

In fact, the employers' cost of workers' compensation insurance in Michigan relative to the costs for employers in other states improved markedly between 1978 and 1984. These comparative costs were examined in section XII of Burton, Hunt, and Krueger (1985), which focused particularly on costs in Michigan and the other Great Lakes states. Several comparisons of particular relevance are shown in table 7-9.[25] After a long rise in the relative cost of workers' compensation in Michigan from 1958 to 1978, there was a decline of 33 percent in workers' compensation costs in Michigan between 1978 and 1984. In 1978, a representative sample of Michigan employers spent 1.89 percent of payroll on workers' compensation insurance premiums, a figure that was 33 percent above the national (26-state) average and 48 percent above the average costs for similar employers in other Great Lakes states.[26] By 1984, after accounting for law changes, experience improvements, and the introduction of open competition into Michigan, this same set of employers spent 1.27 percent of payroll on workers' compensation insurance in Michigan, an amount that was seven percent below the national average and only 19 percent above the average costs for insurance for employers in the other Great Lakes states.

This section examines the reasons for the decline of one-third in workers' compensation costs in Michigan between 1978 and 1984, drawing on material in earlier sections as well as information from other sources. The reasons include the impact of open competition on insurance costs, the influence of statutory amendments that reduced the costs of certain benefits, improving loss experience, and other factors. These influences will be discussed in turn. Then the quantitative importance of each factor will be assessed.

Open Competition

The net impact of open competition on the employers' costs of workers' compensation insurance in Michigan was examined earlier. For the 71 types of employers encompassed by this study, the net impact of open competition (using national payroll weights and Variant II) is estimated as 32.0 percent for 1984 (table 7-5).[27] This percentage represents the different between high adjusted manual rates, which are estimates of the insurance rates that Michigan employers would have paid if the traditional methods of determining workers' compensation insurance charges were still used, and low adjusted manual rates, which are estimates of the insurance premiums actually paid by Michigan employers after allowance for expected dividends.

One assumption that affects the magnitude of the net impact of open competition is that dividends under open competition will be maintained at the level of recent years as shown in table 7-8. A possible consequence of open competition, however, is that dividends will be sharply curtailed, thus reducing the positive impact of open competition. The estimated net impact of open competition in Michigan of 32.0 percent for 1984 must therefore be used with caution. Nevertheless, our conclusion is that the impact of open competition on workers' compensation insurance rates in Michigan during 1984 was substantial, and that the most reasonable estimate of the impact is about 30 percent for 1984.

Benefits

Michigan's experience with permanent disability benefits has changed significantly in recent years. Between 1958 and 1980, the share of all cash benefits accounted for by permanent disability benefits behaved differently in Michigan than in most other states. For example, in all the Great Lakes states with available data, the share accounted for by permanent disability benefits had increased on average by five percentage points (from 57 to 62 percent). Meanwhile, in Michigan the share had increased by 28 percentage points (from 41 to 69 percent of all cash benefits).[28] Thus over the 1958 to 1980 period, Michigan stood out among the Great Lakes states as the jurisdiction with the most rapidly increasing share of the generally expensive permanent disability benefits. This was interpreted by the legislature as a runaway cost situation that had to be reversed.

The amendments to the Michigan statute enacted in 1980 and 1981 appear to have reversed this trend towards the increasing importance of permanent disability benefits so evident in the previous two decades. For example, the share of all cases accounted for by permanent partial disability benefits dropped about 20 to 30 percent after these amendments.[29]

Disentangling the Recent Developments

The data in this study indicate that the costs of workers' compensation insurance for Michigan employers declined substantially between 1978 and 1984. This subsection attempts to disentangle the various factors that explain the decline, including the changes in benefits and the introduction of open competition.

Table 7-10 is based on information included in a recent pure premium document released by CAOM. The table includes information on all rate changes in Michigan effective between July 1, 1978 and January 1, 1984, the dates for the insurance costs compared in this study. The final column of table 7-10 shows the total manual premium level changes that have occurred at various dates between 1978 and 1984. The data in the first three

Table 7-10. Michigan Premium Level Changes Between July 1, 1978 and January 1, 1984 As Shown in Rate Filings

	Percentage Change in Premium for New and Renewal Policies Due To:			
Effective Date	Benefit Change	Experience	Miscellaneous	Total Premium Level Changes
Panel A: Individual Year Changes				
August 1, 1979	3.5	12.1	−1.5	14.3
January 1, 1980	4.9	3.8	−4.5	4.0
January 1, 1982				
Including trend	7.4	−19.8	−0.1	−13.9
(Excluding trend)	(7.4)	(−27.3)	(−0.1)	(−22.0)
January 1, 1983	−6.5	12.9	—	5.6
January 1, 1984	0.3	−9.5	0.5	−8.7
Panel B: Cumulative Changes Through 1984				
1978–1982				
Including trend	16.6	−6.7	6.0	2.3
(Excluding trend)	(16.6)	(−15.4)	(−6.0)	(−7.3)
1983–1984	−6.2	2.2	0.5	−3.6
1978–1984				
Including trend	9.4	−4.7	−5.6	−1.3
(Excluding trend)	(9.4)	(−13.6)	(−5.6)	(−10.6)

Sources: CAOM 1985 Pure Premiums Filing, Appendix C-I-Section D.

columns show the sources of the total manual premium changes, broken down into changes due to benefit levels, experience, and miscellaneous (primarily fund assessments). Panel A of table 7-10 shows data for each date when insurance rates were changed or new pure premium data made available, while panel B shows cumulative changes from 1978 to 1984, broken into subperiods that correspond to the period before benefits were reduced by statutory amendments and the 1983–1984 period when the lower benefits produced by the 1980–1981 amendments were reflected in the insurance rates.

The benefit changes in table 7-10 represent the actuarial estimates of the likely impact on future benefit payments of statutory amendments affecting the weekly amounts, durations, or (in some instances) eligibility rules for indemnity or medical benefits. As shown in panel B of table 7-10, the statutory amendments reflected in the rates that took effect between 1978 and 1982 are estimated to have increased the costs of workers' compensation by a total of 16.6 percent. Then the situation changed in Michigan; the benefit changes reflected in the 1983 and 1984 insurance rates are estimated to have reduced costs by 6.2 percent. The consequence is that over the entire 1978 to 1984 period, statutory amendments are estimated to have increased workers' compensation costs by 9.4 percent.

The experience entry in table 7-10 represents the actuarial judgment about the adjustment in premiums needed because of previous experience under the law. If the actual losses have exceeded the amount of losses expected when the previous insurance rates were set, then the new rates are normally increased by the amount of the experience factor. Conversely, better-than-expected experience under previous rates will lead to a reduction in future rates. As indicated in table 7-10, the previous experience underlying the 1979 and 1980 changes in insurance rates had been unfavorable, resulting in substantial increases in rates.

The context of the substantial reduction in rates in 1982 was unusual and warrants additional discussion. The legislature had mandated a 20-percent reduction in manual rates, and the industry responded with a "voluntary" 22-percent reduction. One reason for this large decrease was the mandated removal of the trend factor (an actuarial adjustment normally used in setting rates) from the experience factor. Since the trend factor is normally used to establish rates in the actuarial procedure in most states, we recalculated the experience factor for 1982 with trend included. The trend factor is included in the simulated manual rates for Michigan that were developed earlier, since our purpose is to estimate what the insurance rates *would have been* in Michigan if the traditional rate-making procedure were still in use.

In addition, the 1982 rate filing cited a drastic drop in expected costs for permanent disability cases, presumably because of the aggressive coordination of benefits provisions of the 1981 reforms. Unfortunately, it is not posible to determine how much influence the targeted 20 percent reduction had on the evaluation of the experience factor in 1982. On a cumulative basis, the experience factor (including the normal trend adjustment) would have produced a 6.7 percent reduction in rates from 1978 to 1982, a 2.2 percent increase in rates in 1983 and 1984, and a 4.7 percent reduction in rates over the entire 1978 to 1984 period (table 7-10, panel B). The miscellaneous entry in table 7-10 represents changes in items such as assessment for special funds. This factor by itself would have produced a 5.6 percent reduction in rates over the entire 1978 to 1984 period.

The benefit change, experience, and miscellaneous factors combine to produce the total manual premium (or pure premium) level changes shown in the final column of table 7-10. Including the traditional trend factor, Michigan insurance rates would have increased by 2.3 percent from 1978 to 1982 and would have declined by 3.6 percent in the next two years. Over the entire 1978 to 1984 period, rates would have declined by 1.3 percent following the traditional procedure to established manual rates.

This relatively small figure of a 1.3-percent reduction in rates is much smaller than the overall reduction in workers' compensation insurance costs in Michigan that we have identified in this study. As shown in panel A of table 7-11, the adjusted manual rates actually dropped by 36.8 percent between July 1, 1978 and January 1, 1984. The balance of table 7-11 attempts to reconcile these large differences.

The factors that would have influenced manual rates in Michigan between 1978 and 1984 are included in the first section in panel B of table 7-11. These are a recapitulation of the factors shown in table 7-10 and would have produced a 1.3-percent reduction in manual rates. The next section in panel B indicates that about 1.0 percent of the overall reduction in insurance rates between 1978 and 1984 can be attributed to the national experience with an increasing impact of dividends, premium discounts, and the other factors that are used to modify manual rates in order to produce high adjusted manual rates.[30] The third entry in panel B shows that open competition produced a net reduction of 32.0 percent in Michigan insurance rates, which represents the 1984 difference between high adjusted manual rates and low adjusted manual rates (table 7-5, Variant II).

If these three sources of rate reduction shown in panel B are combined, the estimated overall rate reduction is 34.7 percent. The figures in panels A and B are derived independently and do not exactly agree, since the reduction in adjusted manual rates shown in panel A of 36.8 percent slightly

Table 7-11. Michigan Employers' Costs of Workers' Compensation Insurance: Changes Between 1978 and 1984

Source of Change		Percentage Change
Panel A: Changes in Adjusted Manual Rates		
Adjusted Manual Rates for 71 Types of Employers in Michigan		
July 1, 1978 (79 equivalent classes)	$2.493	
January 1, 1984 (Low)	$1.576	
Change		−36.8%

Panel B: Estimated Sources of Change in Adjusted Manual Rates		
Factors Affecting Manual Rates		
(1) 1983–1984 Benefit Changes	−6.2%	
(2) 1978–1982 Benefit Changes	16.6%	
(3) 1978–1984 Experience (excluding trend)	−4.7%	
(4) 1978–1984 Miscellaneous	−5.6%	
Total		−1.3%
Factors Affecting High Adjusted Manual Rates		
High Adjusted Manual Rates as Proportion of Manual Rates		
National 1978	.820	
National 1984	.798	
Change		−2.7%
Factors Affecting Low Adjusted Manual Rates		
Net Impact of Open Competition in 1984		−32.0%
(Variant II)		
Cumulative Impact of Sources of Change		
$[1 - (.987 \times .973 \times .68)] \times 100$		−34.7%

Sources: Panel A: 1978 data from Elson and Burton (1981); 1984 data from table 5 of this chapter; Panel B: data from tables 5 and 10 of this chapter.

exceeds the cumulative reduction of 34.7 percent in panel B. This difference is small enough, however, for us to believe we have identified the major sources of the reduced insurance costs in Michigan between 1978 and 1984 with reasonable accuracy. In other words, we conclude that the overwhelming determinant of the lower workers' compensation insurance costs in Michigan was the imposition of open competition, rather than the other changes experienced.

Table 7-11 and the preceding text may suggest a degree of precision in these estimates that we do not intend. Underlying these figures are a number of assumptions that we have made to produce estimates (such as the net impact of open competition on insurance costs) and that actuaries and others have made about the past and future costs of the benefits in the Michigan workers' compensation program. For relatively recent changes, such as the savings to employers from the statutory coordination of benefits, the estimates must also be understood as very speculative. It is clear that the consequences of these statutory changes in benefits have not yet worked their way through the actuarial data used to set rates in administered pricing states.

The estimated savings to Michigan employers shown in table 7-11 must thus be understood as a rough guide to the consequences of the introduction of open competition and of the recent statutory changes in benefits. While we do not purport to defend the exact figures in table 7-11, we are convinced that Michigan employers have benefited substantially from the introduction of open competition and from the statutory changes in benefits. As a result, the employers' costs of workers' compensation insurance in Michigan have been reduced from a level in 1978 that was well above the national average and the average in the other Great Lakes states to a level in 1984 that was close to the national average and much more in line with the average costs in the other Great Lakes states.

Open Competition in Other States

The discussion of the impact of open competition on workers' compensation costs in Michigan is rather extensive, because Michigan is the main concern of this study and because data for the other seven states with open competition in effect by 1984 are more sparse. However, there is a keen policy interest in determining whether the substantial impact of open competition in Michigan is exportable. That is, can any state expect to be able to achieve savings of ten to 30 percent in workers' compensation insurance costs by implementing an open competitive rating law like Michigan's? This section provides a peliminary answer to this question by producing rough estimates of the net impact of open competition in several other states.

The estimated impact of open competition on the cost of workers' compensation insurance in Michigan for the broadest group of employer classifications was about 30 percent in 1984, declining to about ten percent by 1985. This estimate is based on a comparison between the high and low adjusted manual rates shown in table 7-4 and 7-5. The procedure used to devleop high adjusted manual rates must be emphasized since it affects the results. First, manual rates were simulated by using the pure premiums in effect in Michigan on January 1, 1984 and increasing them by the historical loading factor to produce rates that would be fully adequate from an actuarial standpoint under the traditional rate-making approach. After adjustment for the effects of premium discounts, experience rating, dividends, and other factors that traditionally have reduced the employers' costs of workers' compensation insurance, these simulated rates were compared to actual rates charged in the various years.

The eight states with open competition in effect on January 1, 1984 are catalogued in table 7-12. The problem is that there is no guarantee that the manual rates effective in these states on January 1, 1984 were fully adequate from an actuarial standpoint (other than for Michigan, where the simulated manual rates were constructed so as to insure this result). Thus it would be inappropriate to assume that the net impact of open competition in the other seven states would be equivalent to the 30 percent impact in Michigan.

Data provided by the National Council on Compensation Insurance have been used to make rough estimates of the net impact of open competition on insurance rates in the seven other states with open competition for 1984. The NCCI data in table 7-12 show the impact of rate deviations, schedule rating, and dividends on premiums, and the values in columns (5), (7), and (8) have been used in a simple formula to produce the estimated impact of open competition shown in column (9).

Rate deviations and schedule rating (columns (5) and (7)) reduce the employers' costs of workers' compensation at the beginning of the policy period. To the extent that these ex ante reductions reduce the reserves and profits of carriers below acceptable levels, it can be expected that dividends will be reduced. Specifically, in the absence of open competition, dividends could be expected to be at or near the national average of 11.3 percent of net earned premium for 1983. However, if rate departures and schedule rating deplete reserves and profits below normally acceptable levels, then dividends can be expected to be reduced below their normal level. The net influence of open competition thus is the impact of rate departures (column (5)), plus the impact of schedule rating (column (7)), plus the impact of dividends (column (8)), minus the average rate of dividends (11.3 percent).

This formula has the virtue of being responsive to the adequacy of the manual rates that serve as the starting point for determining the net impact of open competition. That is, if a state has generally inadequate rates before implementing open competition, then the net impact of open competition can be expected to be less than the net impact of open competition in a jurisdiction with adequate rates. Rhode Island provides an extreme

Table 7-12. Estimated Net Impact of Open Competition on Workers' Compensation Costs in Eight States With Open Competition in Effect on January 1, 1984

| State (1) | Effective Date of: | | Impact of Rate Departures on: | | Impact of Schedule Rating on: | | Impact of Dividends on Net Earned Premium (8) | Estimated Net Impact of Open Competition (9) |
	Open Competition (2)	Rates in Use on January 1, 1984 (3)	Standard Earned Premium (4)	Net Earned Premium (5)	Standard Earned Premium (6)	Net Earned Premium (7)		
Arkansas	6/17/81	4/1/81	0	0	6.6	7.5	6.6	2.8
Georgia	1/184	1/1/82	7.6	8.6	4.4	5.0	5.5	7.8
Illinois	8/18/82	1/1/84	4.6	5.2	11.8	13.4	5.1	12.4
Kentucky	7/15/82	1/1/84	2.9	3.3	4.0	4.6	5.8	2.4
Michigan	1/1/83	1/1/84	11.5	13.1	7.6	8.6	15.5	25.9
Minnesota	1/1/84	2/1/83	0.2	0.2	3.7	4.2	6.7	−0.2 or 0
Oregon	7/1/82	1/1/84	29.4	33.4	0.0	0.0	11.7	33.8
Rhode Island	9/1/82	9/11/82	0.3	0.3	2.3	2.6	4.1	−4.3 or 0

Sources: Information in column (2) from sources indicated in source note to table 7-1. Information in columns (4), (6), and (8) from "Competitive Pricing—1983," a November 6, 1984 Exhibit prepared by the National Council on Compensation Insurance. The Michigan entry in column (4) has been adjusted to reflect a 13.9-percent trend factor not considered by the NCCI in preparing the Michigan data; the adjustment procedure is based on a conversation with Barry I. Llewellyn, Assistant Secretary, NCCI. The figures in columns (5) and (7) were calculated by John Burton in January, 1985 by dividing the figures in columns (4) and (6) by .879, the ratio between net earned premiums and standard earned premiums shown in table 8 of Burton, Hunt, and Krueger (1985). The figures in column (9) are the sum of the figures in columns (5), (7), and (8) minus 11.3, which is the figure for 1983 dividends as a percentage of net earned premiums shown in table 8, panel A of this chapter.

139

example of the net impact of open competition on rates that are considered inadequate by the insurance industry. The rates in use on Jaunary 1, 1984 had become effective on September 11, 1982. By early 1984, these rates were considered so low by traditional actuarial standards that the National Council on Compensation Insurance made a rate filing indicating that manual rates would have to be increased by 87.8 percent above the September 1982 rates in order to satisfy the traditional requirements for adequacy.

As shown in table 7-12, the estimated net impact of open competition in Rhode Island was minus 4.3 percent. This figure means that the net impact of open competition in Rhode Island as of January 1, 1984 was estimated as zero given the low level of manual rates in use in Rhode Island as of that date. Several of the other states shown in table 7-12 also warrant additional comment. The net impact of open competition in Kentucky may reflect in part the substantial assessments for the special fund that cannot be included in the manual rates. Oregon shows the largest net impact of open competition, but the figure probably reflects another important factor, namely the extent of rate departures initiated by the state fund. Prior to the introduction of open competition in Oregon in 1982, the state fund was already deviating form manual rates by 29 percent. Thus, the overall figure of 33.8 percent for Oregon should be understood as the combined effect of open competition and aggressive pricing by the state fund.

We undoubtedly are only stating the obvious, but the figures in column (9) of table 7-12 must be considered rough estimates of the net impact of open competition on workers' compensation costs in the eight jurisdictions with open competition in effect on January 1, 1984. We are encouraged that the figure for Michigan shown in table 7-12 (25.9 percent) is reasonably close to the figures shown in table 7-5 (29.7 to 32.0 percent), which were developed by an entirely different methodology. However, the lesson of table 7-12 is clear. The impact of open competition on workers' compensation insurance rates depends very much on whether those rates were actuarially adequate before the imposition of open competition.

Conclusions

Although the data for other states with open competition indicate that salutary consequences are not inevitable, it would seem that the confidence that Michigan legislators placed in free and open competition in setting workers' compensation insurance rates was well placed. There has been a clear and very substantial saving for Michigan employers, beginning at about 25 percent in 1983, growing to about 30 percent in 1984, and declining to about ten to 15 percent in 1985. Further, this has been achieved apparently without unduly impacting benefits for injured workers in Michigan. Limited evidence from the Michigan Department of Labor indicates that a long-term trend toward self-insurance has also been reversed by these deep cuts in workers' compensation insurance costs. In 1983 and 1984, there was a small flow of self-insured employers back into the workers' compensation insurance market.[31]

Despite evidence that the savings may be dissipating with the passage of time, the "shock effect" of imposing open competition alone must be considered a gain for Michigan employers. We find it hard to believe that the old administered pricing system would have led to such rapid reductions in rates, even if the improving experience data was totally credible. Clearly the mandated reduction in manual rates and the imposition of open competition had their intended effect, at least in the short term.

The real policy question is whether these changes will in any way endanger the health of the workers' compensation insurance system in Michigan. There has been no increase in withdrawals by insurers from the workers' compensation insurance market in the past few years. But these decisions take time and it may be that such a move will develop in the future. The rise in the number of Michigan employers forced into the residual market pool in 1985 is unsettling. Substantial rate increases undoubtedly will be encountered by such employers. On the other hand, with open competition, we can be more confident that market rates are truly not sufficient to justify writing workers' compensation insurance for these employers. Thus, rather than hide the problem in a confusion of regulatory issues, it is now highlighted as a separate public policy issue.

There is another danger that relates to the role of workers' compensation as a social insurance program. If unsustainable price competition causes rates to fall below the danger point, carrier insolvency is only one of the unpleasant side effects. It is also possible that carriers would find it necessary to contest more claims to protect their reserves when operating at high loss ratios. Therefore, the responsibility of the regulatory authorities in an open competitive market must become much more global in nature. Administrative agencies probably will find it necessary to spend more of their time reviewing contested cases. In short, while the free and unfettered market can provide an efficient price setting and resource allocation mechanism, it cannot guarantee socially acceptable results in the larger sense.

Ultimately, it may turn out that the real impact of open competition is simply to speed up the rate of adjustment of market prices to market conditions and underwriting developments. Thus, in Michigan, it may turn out that the unregulated workers' compensation insurance market will show quicker and more rapid price increases when the underwriting cycle turns tighter as well. It seems clear that workers' compensation rates came down faster between 1981 and 1984 then they would have in the absence of legislative intervention. On the other hand, it is likely that they will rise faster in 1985 and beyond as market conditions change as well.

We will have to see the relative price trends through a complete underwriting cycle before we can reach a final judgment as to the utlimate impact of open competition. Regardless of some possible increase in market volatility, however, the confidence policymakers can place in market prices and market results compared to the situation under administered pricing appears to be well worth the risk.

Notes

1 Price (1986), table 3 indicates that private carriers accounted for 59.3 percent of benefits paid in 1984 for regular programs (excluding the Federal black lung program).

2 See Worrall (1986) for an alternative view of the state of price competition in the workers' compensation insurance market.

3 See Bailey (1982) and Countryman (1982) for a debate on the open competition idea and its implementation.

4 Burton, Hunt, and Krueger (1985). See also Burton and Krueger (1986) for more details on methods used to compare workers' compensation rates in different jurisdictions.

5 See Williams (1986), pp. 216–222, for a more complete discussion of rate deviations.

6 Schedule credits became an important factor in the latter half of 1982 in Michigan, just before the transition to open competition on January 1, 1983.

7 Burton, Hunt, and Krueger (1985) was completed in February of 1985, when the National Council on Compensation Insurance could provide no information on the impact of schedule rating on insurance costs. The NCCI has subsequently released information on the impact of schedule rating in the NCCI states beginning with policy year 1981.

8 See Countryman (1982) and Worrall (1986) for spirited presentations of this point of view.

9 See Hunt (1979) for a description of the political situation surrounding the workers' compensation reform debate in Michigan.

10 See Hunt (1986) for a discussion of the specific content of the reform legislation.

11 MCLA 500.2400 (2).

12 At one point, legislative attention centered on a 60-day trigger for the Michigan Accident Fund to become an exclusive state fund, disallowing private workers' compensation insurance altogether.

13 See the Annual Reports by the Michigan Insurance Commissioner on the state of competition for further information.

14 Fragmentary evidence suggests that self-insured employers did not realize the same cost savings. See Burton, Hunt, and Krueger (1985), pp. 118–124, for further detail.

15 Note that there is a change from standard earned premium data for 1982 and 1983 to total estimated annual premium for 1984 and 1985. Thus, exact comparisons between 1982

and 1983 should be accurate, but comparisons between 1983 and 1984 may be affected by the change in the premium measured.

16 This is in addition to the substantial reductions in 1982 that will be discussed in more detail later.

17 The 71 NCCI insurance classes are shown in Burton and Kreuger (1986), table 7-2. NCCI classes 2501 and 2361 are included in Michigan class 2501.

18 The 70 Michigan classes accounted for 71 percent of the covered payroll in the state in 1983, 73 percent in 1984, and 72 percent in 1985.

19 These loading factors were provided by Kevin Clinton, formerly Chief Actuary of the Michigan Insurance Bureau.

20 The use of a $35 expense constant for 1983–1985 is conservative, since a sample of the 12 largest carrier groups showed that half were using a figure greater than $35 in 1984; the range was from $35 to $75. Use of $60 as an expense constant would slightly increase the values for simulated high adjusted manual rates shown in tables 7-4 and 7-5 (since the ratio of standard earned premium with constants to standard earned premium without constants is 1.02 when the expense constant is $60, higher than the 1.012 ratio for a $35 expense constant). The use of a $60 expense constant would produce estimates of the net impact of open competition that are about 0.5 percent higher than the figures shown in tables 7-4 and 7-5. See Burton, Hunt, and Krueger (1985), p. 67.

21 Payroll enters table 7-3 twice in offsetting fashion (steps 4 and 14) and can be ignored.

22 The most recent three years data are used when more current data are unavailable; thus the 0.990 ratio of standard to manual premium in table 7-6, panel A was used for all three years of Variant II.

23 With a $35 expense constant, the overall differential between manual rates and high adjusted manual rates is 78.8 percent, the figure used for Variant I.

24 In the absence of data, we assume that the overall impact of retrospective rating on the rates that employers would otherwise pay is zero. To the extent that retrospective rating reduces (or increases) the premiums actually paid by employers, the actual insurance rates shown for Michigan in this study are too high (or too low) and the estimated net impact of open competition is too low (or too high).

25 Note that these figures are not identical with those in table 7-4 and 7-5, which rely on 70 and 71 insurance classes. Table 7-9 relies on 44 classes because that is the largest number of insurance classes with historically comparable data.

26 The Great Lakes states are defined as Illinois, Indiana, Michigan, Minnesota, New York, Ohio, Pennsylvania, and Wisconsin.

27 National payroll weights and Variant II of the high adjusted manual rates (which relies on national data on premium discounts et al.) are used because these assumptions most closely correspond to the procedure used to produce the rates for the other jurisdictions to which Michigan rates are compared in this section.

28 See Burton and Partridge (1985) for a full examination of comparative benefit levels.

29 Burton and Partridge (1985), table 3-19.

30 For 1984, high adjusted manual rates are 79.8 percent of manual rates (Variant II of table 7-5); the corresponding percentage for 1978 was 82.0, indicating that the differential between manual rates and high adjusted manual rates had increased between 1978 and 1984.

31 Unfortunately, the difficulty in determining what proportion of workers are covered by self-insurance makes this mostly impressionistic evidence. Nevertheless, those who regulate self-insurance in Michigan report a net flow out of individual self-insured status during 1983 and 1984.

Bibliography

Bailey, William O., "Competitive Rating and Workers' Compensation." *Journal of Insurance Regulation* 1 (1983): 1–8.

Burton, John F., Jr., Hunt, H. Allan, and Krueger, Alan B. *Interstate Variations in the Employers' Costs of Workers' Compensation, with Particular Reference to Michigan and the Other Great Lakes States*. Ithaca, NY: Workers' Compensation Income Systems, Inc., 1985.

Burton, John F., Jr. and Krueger, Alan B. "Interstate Variations in the Employers' Costs of Workers' Compensation, with Particular Reference to Connecticut, New Jersey, and New York." In Chelius, James, ed., *Current Issues in Workers' Compensation*, 1986: 111–208. Kalamazoo, MI: W.E. Upjohn Institute.

Burton, John F., Jr. and Partridge, Dane M. *Workers' Compensation Benefits in Michigan and the Other Great Lakes States*. Ithaca. NY: Workers' Disability Income Systems, Inc., 1985.

Countryman, Gary L., "Open Competition Rating for Workers' Compensation." *Journal of Insurance Regulation* 1 (1982): 9–22.

Hunt, H. Allan. *Workers' Compensation in Michigan: Problems and Prospects*. Kalamazoo, MI: W.E. Upjohn Institute, 1979.

Hunt, H. Allan. "Two Rounds of Workers' Compensation Reform in Michigan." In Chelius, James, ed., *Current Issues in Workers' Compensation*, 1986: 55–84. Kalamazoo, MI: W.E. Upjohn Institute.

Klein, Robert W. "Competitive Rating in Workers' Compensation Insurance: Michigan's Experience." *Journal of Insurance Regulation* 5 (September 1986): 79–108.

Price, Daniel N. "Workers' Compensation: Coverage, Benefits, and Costs, 1984." *Social Security Bulletin* 49: (December 1986) 19–24.

Williams, C. Arthur, Jr. "Workers' Compensation Insurance Rates." In Chelius, James, ed., *Current Issues in Workers' Compensation*, 1986: 209–35. Kalamazoo, MI: W.E. Upjohn Institute.

Worrall, John D. "Nominal Costs, Nominal Prices, and Nominal Profits." In Chelius, James, ed., *Current Issues in Workers' Compensation*, 1986: 251–56. Kalamazoo, MI: W.E. Upjohn Institute.

8 INCORPORATING RISK IN INSURANCE GUARANTY FUND PREMIUMS

J. David Cummins

The marketplace in which property–liability insurers operate has become increasingly risky. Recent years have witnessed price competition far more demanding than any experienced since the formation of the insurance cartels earlier in this century. Historically, high interest rates have led to intense competition among insurers for investable funds coupled with demands by policyholders to be given credit for interest on funds held in reserves. The insurance sector has experienced higher inflation than the economy as a whole due to liberalization of jury verdicts, broadened interpretations of contractual terms, and other factors (see Cummins and Nye, 1981). Losses on long-tail lines have become less and less predictable. These forces have increased the volatility of underwriting profits, made insurers more vulnerable to potential financial difficulties, and increased the risk of insolvency.

Policyholders are protected against the consequences of insolvencies by state insurance guaranty funds. Property–liability insolvency funds exist in all United States jurisdictions. Nearly all funds operate on a post-assessment basis, i.e., solvent companies are assessed after an insolvency has occurred to pay losses that cannot be paid from the remaining assets of the insolvent firm. Assessments are a flat percentage of premium volume for all solvent companies.

A strong economic argument can be made that guaranty fund premiums should depend upon the risk of the companies assessed, i.e., each firm's premium or assessment should be proportionate to the risk it places on the fund as a whole. When premiums are not risk-based, stable companies subsidize the operations of more risky firms. In addition, firms are given an incentive to maximize the value of their net worth by increasing their underwriting or investment risk. Higher returns associated with more risky operating strategies accrue to the firm's owners, while the downside risk is borne by the industry as a whole through the guaranty fund.

The analysis of the effects of guaranty funds on a firm's incentives to take risk is based upon modern financial theory. This theory hypothesizes efficient markets, i.e., markets where information is instantly and costlessly available and is immediately acted upon by rational decision makers. A good introductory discussion of efficient markets appears in Sheffrin (1983). A technical discussion of the implications of financial theory for insurance markets is presented in Cummins (1988). The following expands upon and extends the results of that discussion.

In the absence of guaranty funds, insurance firms will be arrayed along a price/risk spectrum with riskier firms offering insurance at lower prices. Policyholders with low risk-aversion will buy from firms with relatively low premiums and relatively high risk. More risk-averse policyholders will tend to buy from firms with higher premiums and lower insolvency risk. Thus, each firm's insolvency risk is priced in the market, and consumers share in the higher expected returns resulting from high-risk operating strategies.

The introduction of guaranty funds significantly changes the assignment of risk in insurance markets. In effect, all consumers are required to buy default-free insurance policies. The costs of default are transferred from the individual consumer to the insurance market as a whole, since surviving firms are assessed to pay the claims of bankrupt companies. If guaranty fund premiums are flat (e.g., proportional to company size), an incentive is created for insurers to adopt high-risk strategies. This is the case because the benefits of a risky operating strategy (higher expected return) accrue to the owners of the firm, while the downside or insolvency risk is transferred to the insurance industry as a whole. This occurs because the market penalty for adopting a risky strategy has been eliminated and replaced with a penalty (the guaranty fund assessment) that is assessed at the same rate regardless of the risk of the firm.

Risk-based premiums would eliminate the incentive to adopt risky strategies by charging each insurer the full costs of the risk it places on the guaranty fund. Thus, high-risk companies would no longer be able to gain at the expense of the pool as a whole. Since firms would be less likely to engage in risky strategies, regulatory monitoring costs would be reduced. The purpose of this paper is to propose a methodology for estimating risk-based premiums for insurance guaranty funds. Insurance company assets and liabilities are both modeled as stochastic processes. The risk-based premium is the value of the guaranty fund's promise to pay the excess of liabilities over assets in the event of insolvency.

The methodology is derived from modern financial theory and has been utilized to estimate deposit insurance premiums for banks. The seminal work in the area was conducted by Merton (1977, 1978). This chapter generalizes and adapts Merton's results to apply to insurance companies.

Previous Research

The international actuarial profession has had a long-standing interest in the computation of insurance company ruin probabilities. This work is closely related to the calculation of premiums for guaranty funds. The extensive literature in this field is summarized in sources such as Beard, Pentikainen, and Pesonen (1984), Buhlmann (1970), and Gerber (1979). In spite of its mathematical sophistication, actuarial ruin theory has been of limited practical applicability. The principal problems are (1) the mathematical intractability of most of the results, (2) the nearly universal tendency to ignore investment risk, and (3) the failure to recognize that insurance companies operate in a market economy where insurance premiums and asset prices are determined by the interaction of supply and demand.

Actuarial ruin theory is mathematically intractable when applied to most realistic insurance portfolios. This is at least partly attributable to its microorientation. The theory begins by deriving the probability distribution of total annual claims for the insurer. The fundamental formula is given below:

$$F(x) = \sum_{k=0}^{\infty} p(k) \, S^{k*}(x) \qquad (8.1)$$

where

$p(k)$ = the probability that k claims will occur during the year, and
$S^{k*}(x)$ = the kth convolution of the severity of loss distribution, i.e., the probability that total claims will be $\leq x$, given that k claims have occurred.

The probability of ruin (insolvency) is then derived as the probability that W_1, net worth at the end of the year, is less than zero. W_1 is given by the following formula:

$$W_1 = W_0 + P - X \tag{8.2}$$

where

W_0 = net worth at the beginning of the year,
P = premiums, and
X = total claims.

Only under extremely restrictive assumptions has it been possible to derive analytical expressions for the probability of ruin, while realistic simulation models tend to be extremely complicated and expensive to develop and run (see Roy and Cummins, 1985). Thus, actuarial ruin models have rarely been applied in practical situations.

As suggested above, a serious problem with actuarial ruin theory is the tendency to focus almost exclusively on underwriting risk. Most insurers are heavily invested in financial assets such as stocks and bonds. Fluctuations in asset values and rates of return could cause a company to become insolvent even if its underwriting operations were profitable. While some of the more recent efforts of actuarial risk theorists have attempted to recognize investment risk (e.g., Pentikainen, 1984), their investment models tend to ignore both the theoretical and empirical findings of modern financial theory.

Actuarial ruin theory is almost totally supply-side-oriented. The assumption is that the company decides upon premium rates independently of any outside economic forces other than those impacting upon the frequency and severity of loss distributions. In fact, insurance prices and asset prices are determined in markets. Convincing evidence exists that both types of markets are highly competitive. Hence, the typical firm has only moderate control over the price of its product and no control at all over the prices of the assets it purchases. The guaranty fund premium too has a market value, which is implied by the risk–return tradeoffs at equilibrium in the market for assets and contingent claims (policies). In order to have the proper incentive effects, guaranty fund premiums should reflect this implicit market value.

Financial ratio analysis is another approach that could potentially be used to develop risk-based premiums. The most prominent financial ratios are those prescribed by the National Association of Insurance Commissioners (NAIC) Insurance Regulatory Information system (IRIS). This system is designed to identify insurers that may be having financial difficulties and thus are in need of "immediate regulatory attention" (National Association of Insurance Commissioners, 1984, p. 3). For property–liability insurance, 11 ratios are applied, measuring various aspects of an insurance company's financial strength. Companies failing four or more of the 11 tests may be designated priority companies by the NAIC and singled out for special regulatory scrutiny.[1]

A more sophisticated approach is to utilize financial ratios in multivariate statistical analyses to predict companies that are likely to fail. Two methods have been suggested: (1) multiple discriminant analysis (Pinches and Treischmann, 1974) and (2) multiple regression analysis (Harrington and Nelson, 1984). These methods are promising and would represent an improvement over the more naive ratio analysis applied by the NAIC.

While ratio analysis is a valuable regulatory tool, it is not a complete substitute for the methodology suggested in this chapter. Even the best ratio analysis can only hope to identify companies that are more likely to fail. It cannot provide accurate estimates of the expected costs of insolvency. The technique suggested in this chapter is designed to produce such estimates.

The Methodology

Diffusion Processes

The premise of the model is that changes in the assets and liabilities of insurance companies can be represented by diffusion processes. A diffusion process is a continuous-time stochastic process, possessing the Markov property, which is (almost always) continuous. (See Karlin and Taylor, 1981.) Diffusion processes have been widely used to represent physical and economic phenomena. Prominent applications have been in the fields of physics, genetics, and financial economics (e.g., options pricing). Diffusion processes do not exist as physical phenomena, i.e., they are always approximations to the processes being modeled. Thus, their applicability depends upon the accuracy of the approximation.

The applicability of diffusions to the modeling of insurance company assets and liabilities is ultimately an empirical question, and much work remains to be done on this area. However, a priori, one can observe that the assumption of continuity is critical. If insurer assets and liabilties depart significantly from continuity, one would not expect diffusions to provide very accurate approximations.

Diffusion processes have been used extensively to model asset returns. The diffusion process typically employed is geometric Brownian motion. This model forms the basis for the modern theory of options pricing and underlies the most sophisticated models of financial markets. (For examples, see jarrow and Rudd, 1983.) Practical applicability is demonstrated by the use of diffusion-based formulae in actual options trading. If the rates of return on individual stocks are sufficiently well-behaved to be modeled by diffusions, the rate of return on an entire portfolio can be expected to be even more amenable to this type of approximation.

The use of diffusions to approximate the rates of change in the obligations of financial institutions has been studied much less extensively. Prominent examples of the literature that does exist in this area are the papers by Merton mentioned above. On the surface, one might reason that the possibility of large losses (catastrophes) would be sufficient to rule out the continuity assumption. However, the portfolios of most insurers consist of large numbers of individual policies, and the exposure from any given policy is a very small proportion of the total. In addition, reinsurance is used to smooth out the fluctuations resulting from large individual losses or a multiplicity of smaller losses during a short period of time.

Thus, as an approximation, a strong case can be made that the rate of change of insurance company obligations can be modeled using a continuous process. The case is even stronger when one recognizes that jumps can be superimposed upon an underlying continuous process to model the catastrophe hazard. The use of jump processes in this context is the subject of another paper by the author (Cummins, 1988).

The Model

As suggested above, the methodology proposed in this chapter models the rates of change in the assets and liabilities of insurance companies using diffusion processes. The principal variables are assets (A) and liabilities (L). Insolvency occurs if $L > A$, and the costs of insolvency are $\text{Max}(0, L - A)$.

The model assumes that the insurer enters into a contractual arrangement with the guaranty fund at the beginning of a specified contract period. The contract period is of fixed length (e.g., one year). The guaranty fund premium is determined and a premium charge is made at the beginning of the period. At the end of the period, an audit occurs. If assets exceed liabilities at the audit date, the company is permitted to continue operating. A new premium is calculated, applying to the next contract period. If liabilities exceed assets, the guaranty fund takes over the assets of the company and discharges its liabilities. The costs to the fund are $L - A$.

Assets and liabilities are assumed to follow lognormal diffusion processes. This implies the following differential equations:

$$dA/A = \mu_A \, dt + \sigma_A \, dz_A \qquad (8.3)$$

$$dL/L = \mu_L \, dt + \sigma_L \, dz_L \qquad (8.4)$$

where

A = assets,
L = liabilities,
dz_A = a standard Brownian motion process for assets,
dz_L = a standard Brownian motion process for liabilities,
μ_A, σ_A = the instantaneous expected return and instantaneous standard deviation of return on assets, and
μ_L, σ_L = the instantaneous expected return and instantaneous standard deviation of return on liabilities.

The asset and liability processes are assumed to be independent, although there is no loss in tractability when considering nonindependent asset and liability processes (see Cummins, 1988).[2]

The processes $z_A(t)$ and $z_L(t)$ are standard Brownian motion. These random variables can be thought of as particles drifting through time. The instantaneous expected value of a change in either z_A or z_L is zero and the instantaneous standard deviation is 1.0. A change in the value of one of the particles over any time interval of length t (e.g., $w(t) = z_A(t + s)$ − $z_A(s)$ is normally distributed with mean zero and variance t.

The processes specified in equations (8.3) and (8.4) (i.e., $A(t)$ and $L(t)$) are *geometric* Brownian motion processes with drift. (They would be ordinary Brownian motion with drift if the left-hand sides of the equations were dA and dL, respectively.) This means that the probability distribution of the change in the value of assets over a period of length t is lognormal with parameters μ_A and σ_A. An analogous statement holds for liabilities.

As mentioned above, the lognormal distribution has been widely used to model rates of return on financial assets. Lognormal distributions also have been widely used in insurance (see, for example, Cummins and Wiltbank, 1983). Cummins and Nye (1981) have shown that underwriting profits in most lines of insurance also are lognormal.

The processes represented by equations (8.3) and (8.4) have instantaneous rates of change equal to μ_A and μ_L, respectively. These rates of change are deterministic (certain). The stochastic component is represented by the Brownian motion term. Thus, in every instant the two processes change by deterministic amounts represented by μ_A and μ_L, and by random amounts represented by the Brownian motion terms. A single realization of each process is graphed in figure 8-1. The distance between assets and liabilities at time 0 is the company's initial equity. Ruin occurs if liabilities drift above assets by the audit date.

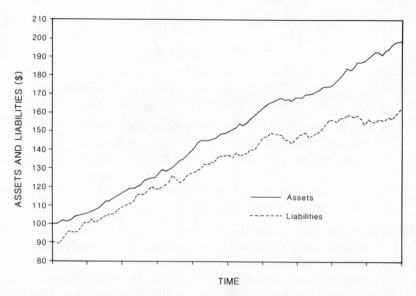

Figure 8-1.   Realization of Assets and Liabilities.

The drift parameter for assets can be defined more fully as follows:

$$\mu_A = r_A + \varrho(N/A) - \theta(L/A) \qquad (8.5)$$

where

r_A = the instantaneous rate of return on the company's asset portfolio,
ϱ = the rate of premium inflow per policy,
N = the number of policies, and
θ = the rate of claim payment per dollar of liabilities.

Thus, instantaneously, assets are increasing because of investment returns and premium receipts and decreasing due to claim payments.

The analogous equation for the liability drift parameter is as follows:

$$\mu_L = \ell - \theta \qquad (8.6)$$

where ℓ = the dollar rate of growth in liabilities per unit time. The parameter ℓ encompasses both monetary inflation in the value of existing liabilities and the dollar rate of occurrence of new claims. It can be decomposed as follows: $\ell = \chi + \eta(N/L)$, where χ is the inflation factor applicable to liabilities and η is the dollar rate of occurrence of new claims. The second term in (8.6) reflects the reduction in liabilities due to the payment of claims.

The guaranty fund premium depends upon the characteristics of assets and liabilities and upon the amount of time remaining until the next audit date (τ). The premium can be represented symbolically as $P(A, L, \tau)$. Implicitly, the premium depends upon the initial distance between assets and liabilities (surplus) as well as the instantaneous rates of change and instantaneous standard deviations of the two processes. Thus, the premium depends upon asset risk and liability risk as well as investment return, premium inflow, claims outflow, and the incidence of new claims.

Stochastic calculus and the theory of diffusion processes can be used to derive a differential equation for the value of the guaranty fund premium, $P(A, L, t)$. The derivation is based on principles of financial market equilibrium and is designed to yield the premium that would occur in competitive markets with perfect information. The equation is an ordinary second-order differential equation, which can easily be solved by numerical methods.

Although the guaranty fund premium equation can be solved without making any assumptions about the relative magnitudes of ϱ, θ, or ℓ, intuitive insights about the process can be gained by making a simplifying assumption. The assumption is merely an expositional convenience and is not necessary to obtain a solution. The assumption is as follows: $\varrho N = \theta L = \ell N$. Thus, premium inflow, claims outflow, and the growth of liabilities are assumed to be equal. Substituting ϱN for θL in equation (8.5), one obtains a process in which assets grow deterministically at rate r_A with random shock term $\sigma_A dz_A$. Substitution of θL for ℓN in equation (8.6) yields a liability process affected only by random shocks ($\sigma_L dz_L$), with no deterministic growth. The assumed conditions may approximately represent a large insurer that has achieved a *steady-state* position.

The simplifying assumption permits one to write the guaranty fund premium equation as follows:

$$.5g_{xx}x^2\sigma^2 + r_f xg_x - r_f g = g_\tau \qquad (8.7)$$

where

$$x = A/L,$$
$$g(x, \tau) = P(A, L, t)/L,$$
$$\sigma^2 = \text{the sum of the asset and liability variance parameters, and}$$
$$r_f = \text{the risk-free rate of interest.}$$

Thus, x is the firm's asset-to-liability ratio, while g is the guaranty fund premium per dollar of liabilities. The premium g is a function of x and τ. Subscripts on g indicate partial differentiation with respect to the variable represented by the subscript.

Equation (8.7) is the standard options pricing equation from financial economics. With the boundary conditions applicable in this case, it is the equation for a put option. An important boundary condition characterizing a put option is

$$g(x, 0) = \text{Max}(0, 1 - x). \tag{8.8}$$

Condition (8.8) indicates that the value of the guaranty fund's obligation (per dollar of liabilities) at the audit date is one minus the asset-to-liability ratio (x). Thus, the guaranty fund incurs a loss only if assets are less than liabilities. The solution of (8.7) subject to the boundary conditions is the following equation (see, for example, Jarrow and Rudd, 1983):

$$g = -xN(y_1) + e^{-r_f \tau}N(y_2) \tag{8.9}$$

where

$$y_1 = -[\ln(x) + (r_f + \sigma^2/2)\tau]/\sigma \sqrt{\tau}, \text{ and}$$
$$y_2 = y_1 + \sigma \sqrt{\tau}.$$

One of the most remarkable aspects of this solution is that the guaranty fund (option) price g depends on r_f, the risk-free rate, and not on r_A, the rate of return on the insurer's asset portfolio. This results from the assumptions that investment markets are in equilibrium and that the guaranty fund insurance is priced to reflect risk in the same way as traded assets.

It makes sense intuitively that the guaranty fund premium can be viewed as the price of a put option. Like the put option, the guaranty fund obligation is a function of lognormal diffusion processes. In addition, the expression for the value of the guaranty fund's liability (which is also one of the boundary conditions) Max(0, 1 − x) is identical to the boundary value of a put with exercise price 1 and asset value x. In effect, the owners of the insurance company can sell the assets of the company to the deposit insurer and in return are released from the obligation to pay the outstanding claims.

As one might expect, $g(x, \tau)$ varies positively with the variance parameter σ^2. Intuitively, a higher variance leads to a higher probability that the option will be exercised (i.e., that the company will become insolvent). The premium $g(x, \tau)$ varies inversely with the risk-free rate r_f. A higher interest rate means that assets are more likely to remain above liabilities. The guaranty fund premium also varies negatively with x, i.e., the premium is less for insurance companies with higher asset-to-liability ratios.

Parameter Estimation and Numerical Examples

Estimation of parameters should be much easier for the guaranty fund model described above than for traditional actuarial ruin models. The simplification results from a top-down or macro approach to approximating the relevant stochastic processes rather than the bottom-up or micro approach adopted in conventional actuarial risk theory. Specifically, rather than starting with frequency and severity processes and using the results as inputs to obtain the distribution of insurer net worth, the present approach utilizes diffusion approximations for the asset and liability processes on a global basis and compares the two processes to determine net worth.

The differential equation for the guaranty fund premium depends upon the drift and risk parameters defined above. Specifically, an operational model without the steady-state assumption would depend upon r_f, ϱ, θ, χ, η, σ_A^2, σ_L^2, and the correlation coefficient between assets and liabilities. The parameters ϱ, χ, and η are growth or trend terms, which can be estimated from the relevant time series. The same time series can be used to estimate the risk parameters. The parameter θ can be estimated by studying a company's claims payout pattern.[3] Obviously, a great deal of work remains to be done to compile and analyze the appropriate time series. The model indicates clearly the types of time series that will be needed and the way in which they interact to determine premiums.

The purpose of this section is to illustrate the calculation of guaranty fund premiums using some rough numerical values of the parameters. The goal is to obtain parameter and premium estimates that are of the same order of magnitude as those that might be obtained in practice. The results are intended as numerical illustrations of the key relationships and do not constitute a test of the model.

Under the steady-state assumption, the guaranty fund differential equation (8.7) utilizes three parameters: (1) the asset variance parameter, (2) the liability variance parameter, and (3) the risk-free rate of interest. The asset and liability variance parameters must be interpreted appropriately in order to derive useful estimates. Recall that these parameters are the coefficients of the Brownian motion terms in the equations for assets and liabilities, respectively. The form of the equations implies that both assets and liabilities are lognormally distributed. The variance parameters thus are properly interpreted as parameters of lognormal distributions of the value-relatives A_t/A_{t-1} and L_t/L_{t-1} where the subscripted variables stand for the values of assets and liabilities at times t and $t - 1$. Thus, the variance parameters were estimated by taking logs of one-year value relatives from a sample of data and estimating the variance of the resulting series.

The data on asset returns were obtained from Ibbotson, Sinquefield, and Siegel (1982). These data cover the period 1926–1980. The data were used to compute variance parameters for common stocks, government bonds, and corporate bonds. The variance parameter for common stocks is

.0437, while the parameters for both types of bonds round off to .003. The asset distribution for stock property–liability insurance companies was obtained from the 1981 edition of *Best's Aggregates and Averages*. The assumption was made that all stocks have a variance parameter of .045, while all other assets have a parameter of .003. Using these assumption, a weighted average variance parameter for the entire portfolio was estimated as .0052.

To estimate the liability variance, total property–liability insurance industry liabilities were obtained from *Best's Aggregates and Averages* for the period 1962–1981. One-year growth rates were calculated, and the logs of the resulting rates were found. The variance parameter was calculated from the latter series. This is analogous to obtaining the value-relatives and then taking logs in the asset return series. The estimated liability variance is .012. The final parameter, the risk-free rate, was initially assumed to be .09. The parameter values are summarized below:

Asset portfolio variance parameter   = .0052
Liability portfolio variance parameter = .012
Risk-free rate   = .09

Sensitivity tests were conducted by varying the parameter values and comparing the results with those obtained using the parameter values given above, which are called the baseline parameter values.

Examples of guaranty fund premiums are presented in table 8-1. Premiums are given for values of the asset-to-liability ratio ranging from .2 to 1.8. As points of reference, the actual asset-to-liability ratio for the entire property–liability insurance industry over the period 1969 through 1982 was about 1.4 (*Best's Aggregates and Averages*) and the average annual guaranty fund assessment during that period was approximately $32 million (National Committee on Insurance Guaranty Funds, 1984). As a ratio to average liabilities over the period 1969 through 1982, guaranty fund assessments amounted to .000307 or .0307 percent.

In interpreting the premiums, one should keep in mind that the variance parameter for liabilities was estimated using industry-wide data. The variance parameters for individual companies are likely to be higher than the parameter for the industry as a whole.

The baseline case is shown in the second column of the table. The estimated deposit insurance premium at an asset-to-liability ratio of 1.4 is .000023 or .0023 percent of liabilities. This is less than ten percent of the average guaranty fund assessment. However, an interest rate of .09 is too high to represent the average rate for the period 1969 through 1982. Re-

Table 8-1.   Guaranty Fund Premiums

Asset Var	.0052	.0052	.0052	.01	.01	.01
Liab Var	.012	.012	.012	.02	.02	.02
Tau	1	1	.5	1	1	.5
RF	.09	.03	.03	.09	.03	.03

A/L	Premium	Premium	Premium	Premium	Premium	Premium
0.2	0.713931	0.770446	0.785112	0.713931	0.770446	0.785112
0.4	0.513931	0.570446	0.585112	0.513931	0.570446	0.585112
0.6	0.313949	0.370449	0.385112	0.313949	0.370554	0.385112
0.8	0.122994	0.174043	0.185466	0.132696	0.180583	0.187100
1.0	0.018313	0.038074	0.029739	0.031698	0.054228	0.041387
1.2	0.000946	0.003140	0.000603	0.004488	0.009918	0.003011
1.4	0.000023	0.000118	0.000002	0.000439	0.001246	0.000086
1.6	3.70E–07	2.63E–06	1.80E–09	3.42E–05	1.22E–04	1.30E–06
1.8	3.60E–09	4.18E–08	1.37E–12	2.31E–06	1.02E–05	1.31E–08

Note: Tau = the length of the contract period, in years; RF = the rate of interest.
ACTUAL ASSESSMENT RATE 1969–1982 = .000307

ducing the rate to .03 increases the premium at the 1.4 asset-to-liability ratio to .00118, approximately 38 percent of the actual assessment. A rate of as low as .03 may be appropriate as an approximation to the difference between investment earnings and the amount paid to policyholders for the use of their funds. (Recall that this is a risk-free, i.e., U.S. government securities, rate.)

As indicated above, the deposit premium is directly related to the variance parameters. Increasing the variance parameter for assets to .01 and the parameter for liabilities to .02 while retaining a one-year contract period and a risk-free rate of .09 yields a guaranty fund premium of .000439 at an asset-to-liability ratio of 1.4. (See column 5 of table 8-1.) This is closer to the actual guaranty funds assessment rate.

The effect of the contract period (τ) on the guaranty fund premium depends upon whether the initial asset-to-liability ratio is less than or greater than one. A ratio less than one implies that the company is insolvent at the beginning of the period, and no guaranty fund would accept such a risk. However, considering ratios less than one is helpful in gaining an understanding of the factors affecting the premium.

If the asset-to-liability ratio is less than one, moving from a one-year to a half-year contract period increases the guaranty fund premium. (See, for example, the last two columns in table 8-1.) The reason is that the fund is almost certain to become responsible for the insurer's liabilities, and the present value of this obligation is greater because the time to the audit date is less. If the asset-to-liability ratio is greater than one, on the other hand, moving to a half-year contract period reduces the premium. This occurs because the potential adverse effects of risk are reduced, i.e., there is less time for liabilities to drift above assets due to adverse fluctuations.

Since the parameters shown in table 8-1 were merely intended as rough estimates of the parameters that might be applicable in practice, it is remarkable that they are of reasonable orders of magnitude when compared to actual guaranty fund assessments. This is encouraging and suggests that more precise estimates may produce accurate guaranty fund premiums.

Conclusions

In this chapter we have proposed a methodology for estimating risk-based premiums for insurance guaranty funds. The methodology is based on the use of diffusion processes and on concepts from the field of financial economics. The premium formula takes into account both asset and liability risk and requires the estimation of only a few parameters.

In addition to its potential value for calculating guaranty fund premiums, the methodology proposed in this chapter may also be useful in testing the financial stability of property–liability insurers. It could serve as a substitute or complement for the NAIC IRIS tests.

Much additional research needs to be done in order to operationalize the methodology. More precise empirical estimates should be developed and extensive tests on data for individual companies should be conducted. In addition, more refined models could be developed that take into account stochastic interest rates, catastrophes, and other risks faced by insurers. This work is underway and will be presented in subsequent papers.

Notes

1 The system is described in more detail in National Association of Insurance Commissioners (NAIC) (1984). The ratios are computed utilizing a computerized data bank maintained by the NAIC. The data bank consists of key variables from the annual statements filed by insurance companies with state insurance commissioners. For each of the 11 audit ratios, a "usual range" has been established by the NAIC "from studies of the ratios for companies that have become insolvent or have experienced financial difficulties in recent years" (NAIC, 1984, p. 2). A team of examiners and financial analysts, representing all regions of the country, meet annually at NAIC headquarters to evaluate the results of the

ratio tests. Special strutiny is given to companies with four or more ratios outside the "usual range." After considering possible mitigating circumstances, the examiners compile a list of companies "requiring immediate regulatory attention." The list is sent to each state insurance commissioner for possible regulatory action. The ratios fall into four major categories: overall ratios (such as premiums written to surplus), profitability ratios (such as investment yield), liquidity ratios (such as agents' balances to surplus), and reserve ratios (such as one-year reserve development to surplus).

2 In real-world applications it would be essential to recognize any correlation between assets and liabilities when estimating guaranty fund premiums.

3 The model implicitly assumes that claims payouts for a block of existing liabilities follow an exponential distribution; i.e., beginning with initial liabilities of L_0, the remaining (unpaid) liabilities at any given time are $L_0 \exp(-\theta t)$, where t is the time since the start of the payout process (i.e., the time when liabilities were valued at L_0). This assumption was also suggested by Kraus and Ross (1982). Preliminary research conducted by the author indicates that the assumption is reasonable for automobile liability insurance claims.

References

Beard, R. E., T. Pentikainen, and E. Pesonen. *Risk Theory*. Third edition. New York: Chapman and Hall, 1984.

Buhlmann, Hans. *Mathematical Methods In Risk Theory*. New York: Springer-Verlag, 1970.

Cummins, J. David. "Risk-Based Premiums for Insurance Guaranty Funds." *Journal of Finance* 43 (1988).

Cummins, J. David, and David J. Nye. "The Stochastic Characteristics of Property–Liability Insurance Profits." *Journal of Risk and Insurance* 47 (1980): 61–80.

Cummins, J. David, and David J. Nye. "Inflation and Property–Liability Insurance." In John D. Long (ed.), *Issues In Insurance*. Vol. 2, second edition. Malvern, PA: American Institute for Property–Liability Underwriters, 1981.

Cummins, J. David, and Laurel Wiltbank. "Estimating the Total Claims Distribution Using Multivariate Frequency and Severity Distributions." *Journal of Risk and Insurance* 50 (1983): 377–403.

Cummins, J. David, and Scott Harrington. "Property–Liability Insurance Rate Regulation: Estimation of Underwriting Betas Using Quarterly Profit Data." *Journal of Risk and Insurance* 52 (1985): 16–43.

Gerber, Hans U. *An Introduction to Mathematical Risk Theory*. Philadelphia: S. S. Huebner Fondation, University of Pennsylvania, 1979.

Harrington, Scott E., and Jack Jelson. "A Regression Based Methodology for Predicting Property–Liability Insurance Company Insolvency." Working paper, Center for Research on Risk and Insurance, University of Pennsylvania, 1984.

Ibbotson, Robert, Rex Sinquefield, and Laurence Siegel. "Historical Returns on Principal Types of Investments." Working Paper No. 71, Center for Research in Security Prices, University of Chicago, 1982.

Jarrow, Robert A., and Andrew Rudd. *Option Pricing*. Homewood, IL: Richard D. Irwin, 1983.

Karline, Samuel, and Howard Taylor. *A Second Course In Stochastic Processes*. New York: Academic Press, 1981.

Kraus, Alan, and Stephen A. Ross. "The Determination of Fair Profits for the Property–Liability Insurance Firm." *Journal of Finance* 37 (1982): 1015–1028.

Merton, Robert. "An Analytic Derivation of the Cost of Deposit Insurance and Loan Guarantees: An Application of Modern Option Pricing Theory." *Journal of Banking and Finance* 1 (1977): 3–11.

Merton, Robert. "On the Cost of Deposit Insurance When There Are Surveillance Costs." *Journal of Business* 51 (1978): 439–452.

National Association of Insurance Commissioners. *Using the NAIC Insurance Regulatory Information System: Property and Liability Edition*. Kansas City, MO, 1984.

National Committee on Insurance Guaranty Funds. "Special NCIGF Report: State Insurance Guaranty Funds and Insurance Company Insolvency Assessment Information." Schaumburg, IL, 1984.

Pentikainen, Teivo (ed.). *Solvency of Insurers and Equalization of Reserves*. Vol. 1. Helsinki: Insurance Publishing Co, 1982.

Pinches, George, and James Trieschmann. "The Efficiency of Alternative Models for Solvency Surveillance In the Insurance Industry." *Journal of Risk and Insurance* 41 (1974): 563–577.

Roy, Yves, and J. David Cummins. "A Stochastic Simulation Model for Reinsurance Decision Making By Ceding Companies." In J. David Cummins (ed.), *Strategic Planning and Modelling In Property–Liability Insurance*. Hingham, MA: Kluwer-Nijhoff, 1985.

Sheffrin, Steven M. *Rational Expectations*. New York: Cambridge University Press, 1983.

Smith, Clifford W., Jr. "Option Pricing: A Review." *Journal of Financial Economics* 3 (1976): 3–51.

9 THE PRICING OF REINSURANCE CONTRACTS

Neil A. Doherty

The derivation of an appropriate price for a reinsurance contract is a formidable problem. This is due in large part to the difficulties encountered in estimating the probability distribution for underlying loss payment. For example, facultative reinsurance contracts on individual direct policies usually apply to the large or catastrophic losses described in the right-hand tail of the loss distribution. But the infrequency of these large losses implies that the tail of the loss distribution is extremely difficult to estimate.[1] Similar estimation problems arise with treaty reinsurance, especially when it is arranged on a nonproportional basis. Despite these problems, some estimate of the loss distribution (or at least of summary characteristics of the distribution) is essential to the derivation of the reinsurance premium. This is true no matter what technique is used to derive an appropriate premium for the reinsurance contract.

A second problem concerns methodology. The procedure used to derive the reinsurance premium should reflect the economic cost imposed by the contract (including, but not limited to, the prospective loss payment) and presumably should reflect the corporate objectives of the participating firms. This second problem is addressed here. One can argue that actuarial methods currently expounded are based on suspect economic foundations.

161

Alternative models based on the Capital Asset Pricing Model and the Arbitrage Pricing Model will be discussed, though we suggest these may encounter operational difficulties. Finally, an option pricing approach to valuation of reinsurance contracts will be presented that is based on more solid economic foundations than the actuarial models but that avoids the more serious estimation problems of the models based upon capital asset pricing theory.

The option approach to reinsurance valuation is generic. There is a set of option models that are motivated by different valuation relationships and that apply to different types of payoff structures. Consequently there is no unique model for valuation of reinsurance contracts. One such model will be presented that may be used to value simple nonproportional reinsurance contracts. More complex valuation models may be developed that cope both with different payoff structures and with the prospect of default on the part of the reinsurer. Such models are not developed here, although directions for their development are suggested.

Actuarial Reinsurance Pricing Methods

Current actuarial methods used for premium calculation appear to be motivated by the insurer's assumed aversion to risk and/or by the insurer's desire to avoid ruin. There is in fact considerable overlap between these ideas. To illustrate, consider figure 9-1, which shows a loss distribution representing the prospective loss payments on either a direct or reinsurance policy. The expected value of loss is $\bar{L}$.

One immediate and obvious requirement for any adequate premium is that it must cover the insurer's expenses. Since expenses cause no particularly difficult problems, we will take it as given that an expense loading will be included. Subject to this expense loading, a premium of $\bar{L}$ is, at face, sufficient to yield a long-run break-even position for the insurer. In fact, a further qualification is needed. Since the timing of the insurer's cash flows do not coincide, the break-even or "pure" premium is equal to the discounted value of losses. Thus, on the fundamental economic principle of the time value of money, we accept as axiomatic the relevance of investment income for premium calculation. For the time being, the random loss described in figure 9-1 may be thought of on a present-value basis. Thus to repeat, subject to these qualifications, the break-even premium is the expected loss $\bar{L}$.

Now consider that the insurer exhibits a distaste for risk or is "averse to risk." It follows that the insurer's welfare would decline if it accepted a

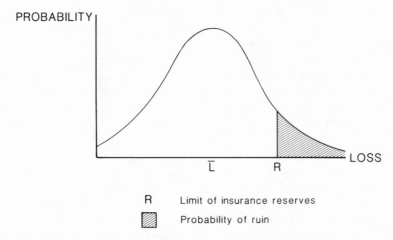

R Limit of insurance reserves

▨ Probability of ruin

Figure 9-1. Loss distribution representing the prospective loss payments on either a direct or reinsurance policy.

policy at premium $\bar{L}$. By accepting the policy, the insurer is substituting an uncertain outcome for a certain outcome with the same expected value. Since risk has negative value, the premium required to make the policy acceptable to the insurer must be positively related to the risk (however measured) and must exceed the pure premium $\bar{L}$.

$$P = f[\bar{L}; \text{RISK}] \qquad (9.1)$$

where

$$P = \text{required premium,}$$
$$f'_{\bar{L}} > 0, \qquad f'_{\text{RISK}} > 0, \qquad \text{and}$$
$$\text{RISK} = \text{a chosen measure of risk.}$$

Examples of risk measures that may be used are the variance, the standard deviation, the semivariance and the relationship between $\bar{L}$ and the maximal loss. A recent description of the properties of these functions is given by Goovaerts, de Vylder and Haezendonck (1984). If the premium structure defined by equation (9.1) is designed to compensate the risk-averse insurer for the riskiness of the policy, it is reasonable to set f(·) according to the insurer's degree of risk aversion.

Another approach in determining premiums related to the insurer's degree of risk aversion is to set premiums that leave the insurer indifferent with regard to accepting or not accepting the policy. This requires that the insurer's utility function be known. In practice this is not the case.

Nevertheless, premium structures derived on this principle are expounded. Examples (see Goovaerts et al., 1984) are the zero utility principle and the Orlitz principle.

Now consider the setting of premiums according to the ruin probability. The loading now may be thought of as a safety loading. Considering the insurer's aggregate liability portfolio, the higher the safety loading the larger the reserve funds and the lower the probability of ruin. The usual approach is to set the premium in order to maintain the ruin probability at some acceptable level. If this approach is used for treaty reinsurance, the premium may be related to the risk level as described by equation (9.1) since the ruin probability is in turn related to the degree of risk in the portfolio. Thus, risk-related premiums may serve the dual purpose of compensating the insurer for the risk it accepts and providing a safety loading related to the ruin probability.

The general principles of premium calculation outlined here have been applied both to direct policies and to reinsurance policies. In fact, these ideas are probably best applied to treaty reinsurances written on the insurer's direct liability portfolio. Relating the premiums of individual policies to the individual policy risk makes little sense since that risk is largely diversified away in the insurer's portfolio. Thus, even if the insurer is risk-averse the individual policy risk is of little relevence. For the same reason, the contribution of an individual policy to the ruin probability of an insurer is not well measured by the standard deviation (or similar risk measure) of that policy.

But if this reasoning is taken further, it will be realized that these principles for calculating premiums are based on tenuous economic logic even when applied to reinsurance. First, the idea that the insurance firm is averse to risk is meaningless. Individuals may be averse to risk, but a firm is not an individual. Rather, the firm is a legal entity created to bring together various parties with different economic functions; customers, managers, suppliers, workers, owners of capital, etc. The firm is the nexus of these contracts; in short, it is simply a market.[2] As it is meaningless to think of a market as being risk-averse, it is meaningless to consider the firm to be risk-averse.

A second problem with these premium calculation methods is that they do not properly consider the process of diversification. Suppose that the owners (shareholders) of the firm are risk-averse and that decisions are made to maximize their welfare. Setting premiums according to policy risk, or even to the risk of the entire liability portfolio, is inappropriate since this risk may be quite unrelated to the risk borne by the shareholders. Shareholders may be able to reduce any risk undertaken by the insurer in the management of their personal investment portfolios. Shareholders would only require compensation for risk that cannot be diversified in this manner—so-called systematic risk.

Adoption of an acceptable ruin probability as an alternative corporate goal does not coincide with current economic thought. The probability of ruin may form an effective constraint on a firm's decision choices, by reason of regulations (e.g., regulations of premium-to-surplus ratios). Furthermore, the probability of ruin may well influence economic performance since the demand for insurance will rationally be related to default risk. But these statements do not imply that minimization of ruin is an all-important corporate objective. A more acceptable objective function (such as profit maximization or value maximization) is required.

Models based on asset pricing theory are now presented. These models specifically address the issues of portfolio diversification and corporate objectives that have been raised.

The Capital Asset Pricing Model (CAPM) and Arbitrage Pricing Model (APM)

Asset pricing models such as these may be used to establish equilibrium prices for insurance or reinsurance contracts.[3] The equilibrium price is essentially that which would prevail under conditions of competition both in the capital market and in the market for insurance services. The interesting feature of insurance prices derived in this way is that they imply that equityholders will receive a competitive expected rate of return on their capital investment in the insurance firm. Consequently, these models may be used to derive a fair price for insurance for the purposes of regulation. The CAPM and other models used for regulatory purposes were surveyed in Cummins (1984; see also Hill, 1979; Hill and Modigliani, 1981; and Fairley, 1979).

The concept of a fair or competitive price is especially useful when considering the pricing of reinsurance contracts. Such a price would give the equityholders of the reinsurer a competitive or fair return on the surplus committed to underwrite the reinsurance contract. Thus the reinsurer has an incentive to maintain its supply of capital and thereby to maintain an acceptably low ruin probability. At the same time, the competitive price, by definition, is insufficient to offer the reinsurer any degree of monopolistic profit. Thus the price will be fair to both the ceding firm and to the reinsurer. These considerations imply that models such as CAPM and APM are attractive instruments for deriving reinsurance prices.

For present purposes, we will outline the essential insights of CAPM and simply make comparative statements concerning APM.

CAPM was derived to estimate equilibrium prices for capital assets on the assumption that investors typically hold fairly diversified asset portfolios. In the same way that insurance diversifies the riskiness of individual policies by pooling those policies in a liability portfolio, so a portfolio of stocks, bonds, or the like will eliminate much of the riskiness of the individual assets. Thus it may be supposed that an investor will not be concerned with the riskiness of each asset; rather he (she) will be concerned with the risk of the portfolio. Each asset will be examined in tems of its contribution to the risk of the portfolio, not for its risk when examined in isolation. In an extreme case when all policies or assets are independent, the formation of a very large insurance portfolio or asset portfolio will diversify out nearly all risk. Thus even though individual assets or policies may be risky in isolation, they will contribute negligible risk to the portfolio. In this case, individual policy or asset risk has practically no cost to the owner of the portfolio even though the owner may be risk-averse. The portfolio owner will not require compensation for bearing the risk associated with individual items.

The case when assets or policies are independent is a special case. More often, assets exhibit some correlation and, while risk is reduced through pooling, it may not be eliminated. For example, a portfolio of policies covering weather-related damage will exhibit positive correlation, since the same weather conditions will simultaneously affect the probability of loss on all policies within the relevant geographic area. Similarly, the returns on financial assets held in an asset portfolio usually exhibit some tendency to move in sympathy with movement of the market as a whole. The correlation with the market is not perfect; there is also some idiosyncratic movement in individual stock returns. Thus we may view the variability of asset returns as divided into two components:

(a)   Unsystematic risk. This is not associated with movements in the aggregate market portfolio of all assets. This risk is easily diversified away by holding a portfolio with a sufficient number and spread of assets.

(b)   Systematic or market risk. This is defined by the size of the correlation between individual stock returns and the market portfolio. Since this represents the common movement of assets, this risk is not diversified away simply by holding a number of assets in a portfolio.

With this division of risk, the CAPM is easily understood. The unsystematic risk of each security imposes little or no cost on the investor since this risk is diversified easily simply by holding a portfolio of securities. But systematic risk, as measured by the security beta, does not diversify away. The security beta measures the contribution of that security to portfolio risk. Since this risk is relevant to the investor, securities with a high beta must offer investors a higher expected rate of return to compensate for added portfolio risk. Lower beta securities contribute little risk to the investor portfolio and therefore will be priced to yield a lower expected rate of return. In equilibrium, the expected rates of return of securities will be linearly related to their betas.

$$E(r_i) = r_f + \beta_i[E(r_m) - r_f] \qquad (9.2)$$

where

$E(\cdot)$ is the expectations operator,
r_i is the return on security i,
r_m is the return on the market index or portfolio,
r_f is the risk-free rate, and

β_i is the security beta defined as $\beta_i = \dfrac{\mathrm{Cov}(r_i r_m)}{\sigma^2(r_m)}$.

Now the CAPM may be used to derive the fair or competitive price for a reinsurance contract. The method is to derive the price (or rate of expected underwriting profit) that will yield the expected rate of return on equity defined by equation (9.2) above. The derivation is routine and the result is (For details see Fairley, 1979; Hill, 1979; and Hill and Modigliani, 1981)

$$E(r_u) = -kr_f + \beta_u[E(r_m) - r_f]$$

where

r_u is the rate of underwriting profit,
k is the stock of investable funds per dollar of premium income, and
β_u is the underwriting beta.

The underwriting beta is defined in similar manner to the security beta:

$$\beta_u = \frac{\mathrm{Cov}\ r_u r_m}{\sigma^2(r_m)}. \qquad (9.3)$$

As suggested earlier, a reinsurance policy priced to deliver this expected rate of underwriting profit also would offer the reinsurance firm's security-holders a competitive or fair expected rate of return on their equity investment. As such, the model offers an attractive basis for pricing reinsurance contracts although, to our knowledge, it has not been used for this purpose. As shown, the model has excluded the effects of taxation, although this feature is incorporated easily (see Hill and Modigliani, 1981).

The main difficulty encountered in applying the CAPM to insurance lies in the calculation of the underwriting betas as described by equation (9.3). These problems are well known from the application of CAPM to regulatory issues. In essence, the problem is that, to calculate the covariance in (9.3), the capital market's valuation of the return on underwriting is required—not simply the accounting profit. In practice, the accounting profit is often used as a proxy for the market value, and the error involved is not known. These problems are compounded by small samples of observations of r_u and r_m. For applications to reinsurance of a nonproportionate nature, the problems may be even more severe. The relevant covariance is between losses over and above the deductible limit of the policy and the market portfolio. The infrequency of such losses and the availability of annual (or at best quarterly) data gives rise to very serious estimation problems, and it is doubtful whether meaningful beta estimates can be derived. In describing these problems, I am not advocating rejection of CAPM in favor of the actuarial methods described earlier. In my view, the problems with the actuarial methods are fundamental, and probably more severe.

The APM represents a generalization of the CAPM both with respect to the factors considered in the pricing relationship and in terms of the economic process from which the equilibrium relationship is derived. The APM has received considerable attention recently and may indeed replace the CAPM as the main pricing paradigm, although judgment on this score must be reserved for the present. The APM preserves the main economic insights of the CAPM: (a) that unsystematic risk is diversifiable and is not priced, and (b) only nondiversifiable risk is priced. The difference for current purposes is that systematic risk is not measured with respect to a single factor, i.e., the market portfolio. Instead, the APM permits risk to be priced in relation to any number of factors although the model allows these factors to be determined empirically rather than specifying them in advance. Suitable candidates for these factors may be the market portfolio (as in CAPM), the rate of inflation, national product, etc. The equilibrium rate of return on the security and the implicit rate of underwriting profit on the reinsurance contract are respectively

$$E(r_i) = r'_f + \sum_{j=1}^{n} \beta_{ij}[E(r_j) - r'_f]$$

$$E(r_u) = -kr_f' + \sum_{j=1}^{n} \beta_{uj}[E(r_j) - r_f']$$

where

r_f' is the return expected on a security with zero systematic risk,
r_j is the return on priced factor j, and
n is the number of priced factors.

While this model represents an attractive development from CAPM in explaining the distribution of security prices, the problems of estimating the betas remain when it is used for deriving competitive insurance prices.

In summary, it is argued that the CAPM and APM are attractive theoretic models from which to derive competitive prices for insurance contracts. However, in their application to reinsurance, there are considerable estimation problems. These problems may be overcome by accepting surrogates for the theoretic betas and, at this level, the models represent improvements on the traditional actuarial methods.

An alternative approach to reinsurance pricing is now outlined. This approach may ameliorate some of these problems while preserving the theoretical advantages of a financial economic model. The alternative is to use option pricing.

An Option Model of Reinsurance Pricing

Using CAPM and APM for reinsurance pricing requires that the reinsurance contract be priced such that the return on equity be competitive. This is achieved implicitly by valuing the insurer's or reinsurer's own equity for which the CAPM or APM must be used. The option pricing method works differently. It is a method of derivative pricing. If asset B is derived from, and only exists relative to, another asset A, then a derivative pricing model will estimate the price of B as a function of that of A. Furthermore, with option pricing models, if A is priced to include a risk premium, then no further risk premium need be included in the derivative price of B. The derivative price is known as a Risk Neutral Valuation Relationship. The promise of this method should be obvious. A reinsurance contract is derived from an underlying asset (e.g., the direct insurance policy). If the value of the underlying asset is known, we should be able to estimate a derivative price for the reinsurance contract without further calculation of a risk premium. The characteristics of options will now be described together with well-known pricing relationships. The analogies for reinsurance pricing will then be drawn.

The most common form of options are those written on stocks. The purchase of an option secures the choice to buy or sell the specified stock at an agreed price (the striking price) at some future date (or over some future period). The option to trade at a fixed price clearly has value. Consider for example the option to purchase stock A (a call option) at a fixed price of \$100 in three months time. If the market price at maturity, P_T, is above \$100, the owner of the option can purchase the stock for \$100 and immediately resell for P_T. Thus the profit is $P_T - \$100$. On the other hand, if the price at maturity is less than \$100 the option can be left to expire without being exercised, there being neither gain nor loss. Since the option offers the possibility of gain and no possibility of loss, it is valuable and will be sold for a price. Before examining this price, consider the contingent payoff to the holder of the call option at maturity.

$$\text{Payoff} = \begin{cases} P_T - X & \text{if } P_T > X \\ 0 & \text{if } P_T \leq X \end{cases} \tag{9.4}$$

where

P_T is the terminal price of the underlying asset, and
X is the striking price, or exercise price.

Notice this is precisely the payoff structure encountered in an excess of loss (or deductible) type of reinsurance contract. This is easily seen by substituting P_T for the loss incurred on the direct policy or portfolio and X for the deductible limit.

The main pricing paradigm developed for such call options is that of Black and Scholes. This is based inter alia on the assumption that the terminal value P_T is lognormal. The Black–Scholes price for a European calle option P_O, is

$$P_O = P_S N(d_1) - X e^{-rt} N(d_2) \tag{9.5}$$

where

$N(\cdot)$ is the normal distribution function evaluated at $(\cdot)$,
P_S = current price of underlying stock,
X = striking price,
r = riskless rate of interest,
t = time to maturity,
$$d_1 = \frac{\log(P_S/X) + (r + .5\sigma^2)t}{\sigma \sqrt{t}}$$
$d_2 = d_1 - \sigma \sqrt{t}$, and
σ = standard deviation of continuously compounded rate of return on the underlying security.

Other option pricing models are available to deal with issues of discrete time, stochastic striking prices, dividends, American options, complex and compound options, etc., as well as pricing models for put options which convey the right to sell rather than to buy. The point here is not to summerize these various models, but to reassure the reader that when applying option pricing to reinsurance, many special features can be accommodated by building onto and adapting the basic pricing formula. We shall be content merely to indicate the possibilities for using option pricing.

The primary feature of the option is that it is written on an underlying asset. When it comes to considering reinsurance as an option, we may consider two ways of defining the option using very different candidates for the underlying asset:

(a)   The underlying asset may be considered to be the direct insurance policy in the case of a facultative policy written on a single risk or the whole liability portfolio of the ceding firm if the reinsurance policy is a treaty written on that portfolio. Thus the payment on the direct policy and the reinsurance policy are described in terms of the contractual loss payment on the direct policy $\tilde{L}$ (assuming excess of loss).

direct policy	reinsurance policy
$\tilde{L}$	$\begin{cases} \tilde{L} - E & \text{if } \tilde{L} > E \\ 0 & \text{if } L \leqslant 0 \end{cases}$

The resemblance to the call option payoff is complete.

(b)   A second, and less obvious, way of defining the underlying asset recognizes the reinsurer's ability to discharge its liability under the reinsurance contract. The reinsurer's asset portfolio embodies its reserves together with its surplus. Only if the value of this asset portfolio is adequate will the reinsurer be able to discharge its claims under the reinsurance policies in full. Thus the payoff under the reinsurance policy is

$$\text{PAYOFF} = \begin{cases} \tilde{L}_R & \text{if } \tilde{Y} > \tilde{L}_R \\ Y & \text{if } \tilde{Y} \leqslant \tilde{L}_R \end{cases} \tag{9.6}$$

where

$\tilde{L}_R$ is the contractual payment under the reinsurance policy, and $\tilde{Y}$ is the terminal value of the reinsurer's asset portfolio.

Thus the payoff is essentially the terminal vlaue of the asset portfolio less the payoff on a call option written on $\tilde{Y}$ with striking price $\tilde{L}_R$:

$$\tilde{Y} - c(\tilde{Y}, \tilde{L}_R) \tag{9.7}$$

The virtue of this approach to reinsurance pricing is that it recognizes the default probability of the reinsurer.

Each of the above approaches has its advantages and disadvantages which will be discussed in turn.

Derivation of the Reinsurance Price from the Value of the Direct Insurance Contract

The first of the two methods described above sets a Risk Neutral Valuatin Relationship between the direct and reinsurance contracts. The reinsurance contract valued here is an excess of loss contract written either on a single direct policy or on the liability portfolio of the ceding firm. The option model used here is a discrete time model unlike the continuous time model of Black–Scholes mentioned earlier. There are both theoretical and operational reasons for choosing a discrete time model over a continuous model. The continuous model requires that the holder of the option be able to continuously maintain a perfect hedge. It is doubtful whether this condition could be met in a market where secondary trading of insurance contracts is precluded by the insurable interest requirements. Moreover, the continuous time model requires an estimate of the instantaneous variance of the rate of return to underwriting. Such an estimate will be difficult to obtain and will probably be quite unreliable. Finally, the discrete nature of tax assessments favors the discrete time model.

The model we present is one of two alternative approaches to the problem. Here it is assumed that the distribution for the loss on the direct policy and the wealth of the representative investor are bivariate normal. Furthermore, the representative investor is assumed to exhibit a utility function with constant absolute risk aversion. The normal distribution assumption probably makes this model more suited to portfolio reinsurance where the central limit theorem dictates close approximation to normality if loss correlations are low. However, it may be noted that an alterenative model may be derived with joint lognormality if this is considered to describe the data more accurately.

The model presented here is based upon the discrete time option pricing model developed by Rubinstein (1974) and extended by Brennan (1979) and Stapleton and Subrahmanyam (1984). The derivation will not be presented here, and the reader is referred to Doherty and Garven (1986) for a derivation of a closely related problem. The appropriate price for a reinsurance contract under these assumptions is P_R:

$$P_R = R_F^{-1} X_1 N\left[\frac{X_1}{\sigma(L)}\right] + R_F^{-1}\sigma(L)n\left[\frac{X_1}{\sigma(L)}\right] \qquad (9.8)$$

where

$$X_1 = P\left[1 + \frac{1 - \theta t}{1 - t} kr_F - \frac{1}{S}\frac{\theta t}{1 - t}r_f\right] - D,$$

r_F = riskless interest rate,

$R_F = 1 + r_F$,

t = corporate marginal tax rate,

θt = effective tax rate on insurer's investment income,

k = funds-generating coefficient; i.e., dollars of investable funds generated per dollar of premiums,

S = premium-to-surplus ratio,

D = deductible on reinsurance contract,

P = premium on direct contract,

$N(\cdot)$ = cumulative standard normal density at $(\cdot)$,

$n(\cdot)$ = standard normal density at $(\cdot)$,

$\sigma(L)$ = standard deviation of loss distribution.

Values of θ and S refer to the reinsurer's tax and financial circumstances.

Whether this model is operational or not depends upon the accessibility of data required and upon the generality of the model which is in turn determined in large part by the restrictive assumptions required for its construction. We will examine each issue in turn.

The data required for the model may be classified as follows:

$\left.\begin{array}{l}r_F \\ \\ t\end{array}\right\}$ data not specific to firm

$\left.\begin{array}{l}\theta \\ \\ S\end{array}\right\}$ financial data specific to reinsurer

$\left.\begin{array}{l}k \\ \\ \sigma(L)\end{array}\right\}$ data specific to the loss

P } data on direct insurance contract

The data requirements are fairly modest, and certainly no more burdensome than any reasonable actuarial model. Indeed some of the actuarial models based on utility demand much more formidable data inputs. The only data specific to the reinsured loss are the premium on the direct policy (defined here net of expenses), the estimated standard deviation of loss payment (on the direct policy not on the reinsurance policy), and the funds-generating coefficient. The funds-generating coefficient k may well be estimated from the underwriting results of the firm or industry on similar lines and may be treated thereby as firm or industry data. Notice that the expected value of $\tilde{L}$ is not required, somewhat curiously. However, this value is impounded in the price of the direct contract P, which is assumed to be a competitive price. Thus it is asserted that this approach does not impose serious data requirements relative to other models with less rigorous economic foundation. Certainly the data requirements are no more onerous than for the CAPM and APM, which require the troublesome estimation of betas.

Each of the models earlier summarized in this paper is based on restrictive assumptions. For example, the actuarial models based upon a risk markup assume a typical distributional form for losses which (in many cases) is completely described by two moments, e.g., the normal distribution,[4] and they assume that the owners of the insurance firm possess no other risky assets. Although such assumptions often are not made explicit, they are nonetheless real and severely restrict the application of the model. For its part the CAPM requires, inter alia, conditions tantamount to perfect capital markets in which investors exhibit quadratic utility or for which the final distributions of assets held by investors are normal. Furthermore, this model does not address the probability of ruin when applied to insurance pricing. The option pricing model presented here has its own restrictions. In the form presented, the loss distribution is assumed bivariate normal with the wealth distribution of the representative investor. The representative investor exhibits a utility function with constant absolute risk aversion, though it is not necessary to be more specific on this function. Moreover, the model does not address ruin. Whether these assumptions are more burdensome than other models or more closely approximate reality is a matter of judgment. However, similar option pricing models may be developed on different assumptions which might be judged to more closely fit the dimensions of the problem. In particular, a very similar model can be constructed using bivariate lognormality and constant relative risk aversion on the part of the representative investor.

Derivation of the Reinsurance Price from the Value of the Reinsurer's Asset Portfolio

In the model outlined above the reinsurance price is derived from the price of the direct contract assuming the latter to be competitively priced. But the model does not consider the prospect of ruin on the part of the reinsurer. Development of an option model to accomplish this task is not easy. However, the possibilities for such development will be outlined in the spirit of suggesting a possible direction for future research.

Consider a reinsurance policy written on the liability portfolio of the direct insurer. As a starting point, we suppose this is the only policy written by the reinsurer. This second condition determines that the ceding firm will have the first claim on the assets of the reinsurer that embody its reserves and policyholder surplus. The payoff on the reinsurance policy, as shown earlier, is as shown in equation (9.6):

$$\text{PAYOFF} = \begin{cases} \tilde{L}_R & \text{if } \tilde{Y} > \tilde{L}_R \\ \tilde{Y} & \text{if } \tilde{Y} \leq \tilde{L}_R \end{cases}.$$

This may be valued as equation (9.7):

$$\tilde{Y} - c(\tilde{Y}; \tilde{L}_R)$$

where, as described earlier, $c(Y; L_R)$ is a call option written on the reinsurer's asset portfolio $\tilde{Y}$, with a striking price $\tilde{L}_R$.

In principle, there are no great difficulties valuing this option although it is complicated by the fact that the striking price is itself random. But, as stated, the problem is not too interesting since it pays no attention to the contractual payment on the reinsurance policy $\tilde{L}_R$ and its relationship in turn to the loss payment on the direct policy $\tilde{L}$. We know from the previous model (equation (9.8)) that $\tilde{L}_R$ may itself be valued as an option written on $\tilde{L}$ if the reinsurance policy is of the excess of loss form. Putting these ideas together, the payoff on the reinsurance policy becomes

$$\text{MIN}[\text{MAX}(\tilde{L} - D, O); Y]$$

which is, in effect, an option written on an option. Valuation models for such complex options have been derived in continuous time (Stutz, 1982) and it may be fruitful to pursue their application to reinsurance.

The valuation problem just outlined is quite specific. Of more general interest is the problem in which the reinsurer has a portfolio of reinsurance policies which rank equally with each other in the legal pecking order. This problem too is amendable to appropriate modeling with options. The sketch of a model outlined in this chapter should be sufficient to indicate some possibilities.

Notes

1 Maximium likelihood estimation with censored data has been an effective means of estimating the tail of a loss distribution.

2 For an exposition of this view and its implications for management control, see Jensen and Meckling (1976).

For a series of applications of these models to insurance pricing, see the various papers in Cummins and Harrington (1986). See also the monograph by D'Arcy and Doherty (1987).

4 An alternative implication of the two-moment models is that they imply restrictions on the decision maker's utility function; e.g. mean variance analysis is consistent with quadratic utility.

References

Brennan, M. "The Pricing of Contingent Claims in Discrete Time Models." *Journal of Finance* 34 (1977): 53–68.

Cummins, J.D. "Fair Rate of Return in Property–Liability Insurance: A Review of Alternative Methods." National Council on Compensation Insurance Seminar, New York, 1984.

Cummins, J.D., and S.E. Harrington. *The Fair Rate of Return in Property–Liability Insurance*. Boston: Kluwer Nijhoff Publishing, 1986.

D'Arcy, S., and N.A. Doherty. *The Financial Theory of Pricing Property Liability Insurance Contracts*, S.S. Heubner series in Risk and Insurance, University of Pennsylvania: R.D. Irwin, 1987.

Doherty, N.A. *Corporate Risk Management: A Financial Exposition*. New York: McGraw Hill, 1985.

Doherty, N.A., and J.R. Garven. "Price Regulation in Property Liability Insurance: A Contingent Claims Approach." *Journal of Finance* 41 (1986): 1031–1050.

Fairley, W.B. "Investment Income and Profit Margins in Property Liability Insurance: Theory and Empirical Results." *Bell Journal of Economics* 10 (1979): 192–210.

Goovaerts, M.J., F. de Vylder, and J. Haezendonck. *Insurance Premiums: Theory and Applications*. Amsterdam: North Holland, 1984.

Hill, R.D. "Profit Regulation in Property Liability Insurance." *Bell Journal of Economics* 10 (1979): 172–191.

Hill, R.D., and F. Modigliani. "The Massachusetts Model of Profit Regulation in Non-Life Insurance: An Appraisal and Extensions." Massachusetts Automobile Insurance Rate Hearings, Boston, 1981.

Jensen, M.C., and W.H. Meckling. "Theory of the Firm, Managerial Behaviour, Agency Costs and Ownership Structure." *Journal of Financial Economics* 3 (1976): 305–360.

Mayers, D., and C.W. Smith. "On the Corporate Demand for Insurance." *Journal of Business* 55 (1982): 197–223.

Rubinstein, M. "The Valuation of Uncertain Income Streams and the Pricing of Options." *Bell Journal of Economics and Management Science* 7 (1976): 407–425.

Stapleton, R. C., and M. G. Subrahmanyam. "The Valuation of Multivariate Contingent Claims in Discrete Time Models." *Journal of Finance* 39 (1984): 207–228.

Stultz, R. "Options on the Minimum or Maximum of Two Risky Assets." *Journal of Financial Economics* 10 (1982): 161–185.

Index

179